MICROSOFT® *Quick* REFERENCE

MS-DOS® QBasic™

Microsoft
P R E S S
®

PUBLISHED BY
Microsoft Press
A Division of Microsoft Corporation
One Microsoft Way, Redmond, Washington 98052-6399

Library of Congress Cataloging-in-Publication Data

Jamsa Kris A.
    MS-DOS QBasic / Kris Jamsa.
      p.   cm. — (Microsoft quick reference)
    ISBN 1-55615-355-4
    1. QBasic (Computer program language)   2. MS-DOS (Computer
operating system) I. Title. II. Series.
QA76.73.Q33J36   1991
005.26'2—dc20   90-29072
                                            CIP

Printed and bound in the United States of America.

2 3 4 5 6 7 8 9 MAMA 5 4 3 2 1

Distributed to the book trade in Canada by Macmillan of Canada, a
division of Canada Publishing Corporation

Distributed to the book trade outside the United States and Canada
by Penguin Books Ltd.

Penguin Books Ltd., Harmondsworth, Middlesex, England
Penguin Books Australia Ltd., Ringwood, Victoria, Australia
Penguin Books N.Z. Ltd., 182-190 Wairau Road, Auckland 10,
New Zealand

British Cataloging-in-Publication Data available.

Acquisitions Editor: Michael Halvorson
Project Editor: Casey D. Doyle
Technical Editor: Mary DeJong
Editing and Technical Review: Editorial Inc.

Contents

Introduction

This quick reference guide provides specifics on every Microsoft QBasic statement and function. Each entry includes a brief description, complete syntax, details on parameters, and usually a sample program fragment. In addition, this introduction contains information on the QBasic command line options and a general discussion of QBasic types, variables, and operators. The section "Using QBasic" introduces the QBasic environment and explains how to create, run, and edit QBasic programs.

USING THE QUICK REFERENCE

Each QBasic statement and function is described in the following format:

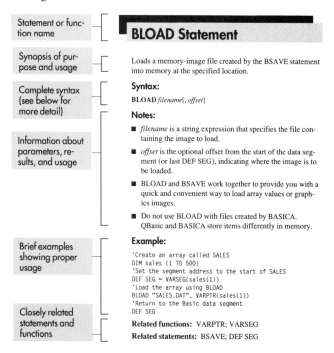

Statement or function name

Synopsis of purpose and usage

Complete syntax (see below for more detail)

Information about parameters, results, and usage

Brief examples showing proper usage

Closely related statements and functions

BLOAD Statement

Loads a memory-image file created by the BSAVE statement into memory at the specified location.

Syntax:
BLOAD *filename*[, *offset*]

Notes:

■ *filename* is a string expression that specifies the file containing the image to load.

■ *offset* is the optional offset from the start of the data segment (or last DEF SEG), indicating where the image is to be loaded.

■ BLOAD and BSAVE work together to provide you with a quick and convenient way to load array values or graphics images.

■ Do not use BLOAD with files created by BASICA. QBasic and BASICA store items differently in memory.

Example:
```
'Create an array called SALES
DIM sales (1 TO 500)
'Set the segment address to the start of SALES
DEF SEG = VARSEG(sales(1))
'Load the array using BLOAD
BLOAD "SALES.DAT", VARPTR(sales(1))
'Return to the Basic data segment
DEF SEG
```

Related functions: VARPTR; VARSEG
Related statements: BSAVE; DEF SEG

1

The syntax lines use the following conventions:

Convention	Description
BOLDFACE	You must enter all boldface characters as shown, unless they are enclosed in square brackets as explained below. Although QBasic does not distinguish between uppercase and lowercase letters, all QBasic keywords appear in uppercase letters when entered in the QBasic environment.
italics	Italicized names are placeholders for information you must supply, such as a filename or a numeric value.
[*item*]	Items enclosed in square brackets are optional.
{*item1* | *item2*}	Braces and a broken vertical bar indicate a choice among two or more items. You must choose one of the items unless the choices are enclosed in square brackets.
item...	Three dots following an item indicate that you can add more items of the same form.
item ⋮ *item*	Three dots in a column between two statements indicate that you can enter additional statements.

COMMAND LINE OPTIONS

You can use the following options when starting QBasic from the MS-DOS command line:

Option	Description
/b	Forces monochrome display
/editor	Starts only the MS-DOS text editor
filename	Loads the specified Basic source file (or text file if /editor used); appends BAS (or TXT for text files) to filename if extension omitted.
/g	Forces faster video output
/h	Forces maximum resolution for the video device
/mbf	Causes numbers to be read and stored in Microsoft binary format
/nohi	Allows the use of a monitor with no high-intensity support
/run *filename*	Runs the specified Basic source file

DIFFERENCES BETWEEN QBASIC AND GW-BASIC/BASICA

	QBasic	GW-BASIC/BASICA
Language Features		
Line numbers	Optional	Mandatory
IF statement	One line or block form	One line
Subprograms	Supported	Not supported
Functions	Supported	Not supported
User-defined records	Supported	Not supported
SELECT CASE statement	Supported	Not supported
DO statement	Supported	Not supported
Long integers (32 bit)	Supported	Not supported
IEEE floating point	Supported	Not supported
Constants	Supported	Not supported
Fixed-length strings	Supported	Not supported
Recursion	Supported	Not supported
Code and data	160 KB	64 KB
System Features		
VGA video modes	Supported	Not supported
Hercules video modes	Supported	Not supported
Olivetti video modes	Supported	Not supported
Cassette tape interface	Supported	Not supported
Mouse interface	Supported	Not supported
Programming Features		
Debugging aids	Supported	Not supported
Instant syntax checking	Supported	Not supported
Windows	Supported	Not supported
Online help	Supported	Not supported
Menu interface	Supported	Not supported

QBASIC HOT KEY SUMMARY

Hot Key Combination	Feature
Shift-direction key	Selects a character
Shift-Ctrl-direction key	Selects a word
Del	Deletes selected text
Ctrl-G	Deletes a character
Ctrl-Y	Deletes a line
Ctrl-Q-Y	Deletes to end of line
Shift-Del	Cuts selected text
Ctrl-Ins	Copies selected text to clipboard
Ins	Toggles insert/overstrike mode
Home-Ctrl-N	Inserts a line above
End-Enter	Inserts a line below
Shift-Ins	Pastes text from clipboard
F4	Shows output screen
Shift-F5	Runs the current program
Ctrl-Q-F	Searches for text
F3	Repeats text search
Shift-F1	Starts QBasic help
F1	Starts help on selected word
F2	Shows subroutine list
F5	Continues execution
F7	Executes to cursor
F9	Toggles breakpoint
F8	Executes a single statement
F10	Executes a single statement or procedure

QBASIC TYPES

Type	Description
INTEGER	2-byte value in the range –32,768 through 32,767
LONG	4-byte value in the range –2,147,483,648 through 2,147,483,647
SINGLE	4-byte value with 7 digits of significance
DOUBLE	8-byte value with 15 digits of significance
STRING	A sequence of up to 32,767 characters

VARIABLE NAMES

A QBasic variable name can contain up to 40 characters (letters, numbers, and periods). In addition, you can append one of the following characters to the name to indicate a specific variable type:

Character	Meaning
%	Integer variable
&	Long integer variable
!	Single-precision variable
#	Double-precision variable
$	String variable

Names reserved for Basic commands, functions, or operator names cannot be used as variable names. QBasic is not case sensitive. (For example, the variable names *count* and *COUNT* are identical to QBasic.)

ARRAYS

To create a QBasic array, use the following syntax:

DIM *arrayname* ([*start_index* **TO**] *last_index* [, ...]) **AS** *typename*

start_index TO *last_index* is the range of index values for the elements of the array. If you omit a starting index, QBasic uses the value 0 by default. (The OPTION BASE statement allows you to set the default starting index.) The three periods indicate that QBasic supports multidimensional arrays.

You can specify up to 60 dimensions. For example, the following statement creates a two-dimensional array with 3 rows and 5 columns:

```
DIM box (1 TO 3, 1 TO 5) AS INTEGER
```

typename is the type of the array: INTEGER, LONG, SINGLE, DOUBLE, or STRING. The maximum array size is 64 KB. Valid index values range from −32,768 to 32,767.

SYMBOLIC CONSTANTS

QBasic allows your programs to reference symbolic constants that you define with the CONST statement:

```
CONST size% = 255
```

QBasic constant names follow the naming conventions used for variables.

Once you define a constant, you can use it throughout your program:

```
DIM a(size%) AS INTEGER
```

In so doing, you simplify future changes to your program and improve the program's readability.

LABEL NAMES

For programs that don't use line numbers, QBasic allows you to use labels to reference specific locations in the program. A label name can contain up to 40 characters. Label names must begin with a letter and must end with a colon (:). Names reserved for Basic commands, functions, or operator names cannot be used as label names. QBasic is not case sensitive. (For example, the labels Handler: and HANDLER: are identical to QBasic.)

PRECEDENCE OF OPERATORS

QBasic uses the following operator-precedence table when
performing operations in a given expression. Operations at
the same level of precedence are performed from left to right.

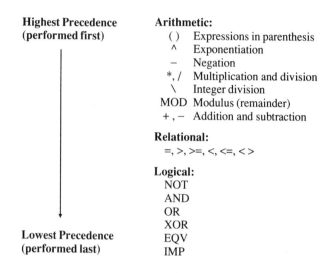

Highest Precedence
(performed first)

Arithmetic:

( )	Expressions in parenthesis
^	Exponentiation
−	Negation
*, /	Multiplication and division
\	Integer division
MOD	Modulus (remainder)
+ , −	Addition and subtraction

Relational:

=, >, >=, <, <=, < >

Logical:

NOT
AND
OR
XOR

Lowest Precedence   EQV
(performed last)   IMP

SUBROUTINES AND FUNCTIONS

The maximum QBasic subroutine size is 64 KB. You can
pass up to 60 parameters to a subroutine. You can create
subroutines and functions using the SUB and FUNCTION
statements.

DATA FILES

QBasic data files can be as large as the available space on
your disk. You can use the file numbers 1 to 255. The largest
possible record size for a random-access file is 32,767 bytes.
The largest possible record number is 2,147,483,647.

MULTIPLE STATEMENTS

You can put multiple statements on a single line if you separate them with a colon (:).

Using QBasic

QBasic is a powerful environment for creating, testing, and running Basic programs. Before examining QBasic's advanced capabilities in this section, you will get a feel for creating, running, and changing simple programs.

STARTING QBASIC

Start QBasic by using your mouse to click on QBASIC.EXE from within the MS-DOS Shell or by typing in the command QBASIC at the MS-DOS prompt and pressing the Enter key. If you start QBasic from the MS-DOS Shell, simply press Enter at the prompt for a QBasic filename.

QBasic first displays an introductory screen that prompts you to press Enter if you want to view the Survival Guide, a screenful of tips on QBasic's essential operations. Press Enter to review the tips. When you are done, press the Esc key. QBasic then displays the following screen:

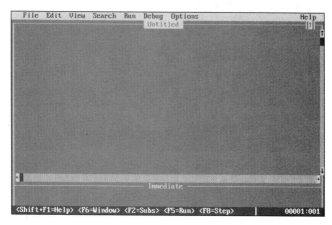

The menu bar, which is displayed in the top row of the screen, contains QBasic's menus (listed on the next page).

- File: Lets you save or print the current program, open an existing program for editing, or exit QBasic to MS-DOS.

- Edit: Lets you easily move or copy text from one location to another or delete text that is no longer needed. Also lets you create new subprograms and functions.

- View: Lets you select a specific subprogram or function for display, divide your screen to view two different portions of a program at once, or view QBasic's output screen.

- Search: Lets you search a program for a specific word or phrase or replace one word or phrase with another throughout a program.

- Run: Lets you run the current QBasic program or continue the program's execution after it has stopped at a debug breakpoint.

- Debug: Helps you locate errors in a program by letting you execute the program one statement at a time. Also allows you to set and clear breakpoints and set the next statement to execute.

- Options: Lets you customize the QBasic screen colors, define the location of QBasic's Help file, and enable or disable QBasic's automatic syntax checking.

- Help: Lets you access the contents, index, or context-sensitive help of the online help system.

To open a QBasic menu, click on the menu name with your mouse, or press the Alt key and the key corresponding to the first letter in the menu name. For example, to open the File menu, press the Alt-F key combination.

Open the File menu. QBasic displays the following drop-down menu:

You can select a menu command by clicking on it with your mouse, pressing the key that corresponds to the highlighted letter in the command name, or highlighting the command name using your keyboard's direction keys and pressing Enter. To remove the menu from the screen, press the Esc key, or click the mouse outside of the menu.

CREATING AND RUNNING YOUR FIRST QBASIC PROGRAM

Type in the following lines, pressing Enter after each one, to create a simple program. (Unlike earlier versions of Basic, QBasic does not require you to type in line numbers before program statements; however, if you like to use line numbers or already have Basic programs that use them, QBasic will support them.) Be sure you type each program statement correctly and enclose the message in the second statement in double quotation marks.

```
CLS
PRINT "Hello, world!"
END
```

The CLS statement clears the screen. The PRINT statement displays a hello message, and the END statement ends the program.

Press the Shift-F5 key combination to run the program. QBasic displays a screen containing the program's output and a message directing you to press any key to continue.

QBasic uses two screens: the environment screen and the output screen. When you are working on a program, the environment screen, which contains the Program window that holds program statements, the QBasic menu bar, and the Immediate window, is visible. When you run a program, the output screen is visible. These two screens allow you to view the program's previous output as you work on program statements. Press F4 to view the output screen.

SAVING A QBASIC PROGRAM ON DISK

After you create a program, you can save it on disk. Open
the File menu and select the Save As command. An ellipsis
after a command name indicates that when you select the
command, a dialog box will appear. When you select the
Save As command, QBasic displays a dialog box that
prompts you to type in the name of your program. In this
case, type in the filename HELLO.BAS as shown:

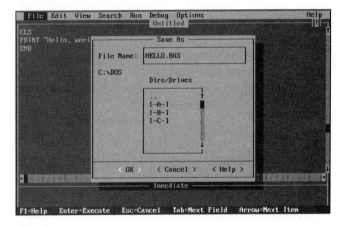

The BAS extension indicates that a file contains a Basic program. The name HELLO describes the program's task (to display a hello message).

Press Enter to save the file's contents. QBasic saves the program, removes the dialog box from your screen, and displays
the program's name immediately below the menu bar.

CREATING A NEW PROGRAM

After you have completed a program and saved it on disk,
you can start a new program by selecting the New command
from the File menu. QBasic will clear the Program window
and label the program Untitled. Type in the statements for
a new program and then save it on disk as previously
discussed.

RUNNING AN EXISTING PROGRAM

To run an existing program or load it into the Program window for editing, select the Open command from the File menu. QBasic displays a dialog box listing the Basic files in the current directory, as shown in the following figure:

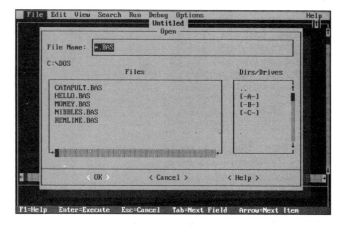

QBasic provides several ways for you to open a program file for editing. First, you can simply type in the program's name and press Enter. (If the program file does not reside in the current directory, type in a complete directory path to the file.) Second, if the filename appears in the list of files, you can double-click on the name with your mouse. Third, you can press the Tab key until the cursor is in the box that lists the filename, highlight the name using the direction keys, and then press Enter to open the file. If the file you want is in a different directory, press the Tab key until the cursor advances to the Dirs/Drives list, select the appropriate directory, and press Enter. When you change directories, QBasic will list all of the files with the BAS extension in the new directory.

In this case, select the program HELLO.BAS that you created earlier. QBasic displays the program's contents in the Program window. Using the direction keys, move the

cursor around the file. As you move the cursor, QBasic
shows the cursor's current line and column position at the
lower right-hand corner of the screen.

EDITING AN EXISTING PROGRAM

With the program HELLO.BAS showing in the Program window, move the cursor to the word *world*. Using the Del key,
erase this word, and type in your own name. After you make
your changes, you can save the program's new contents on
disk using the Save command from the File menu. Unlike
the Save As command, this command saves the program's
current contents on disk using the existing name.

EXITING QBASIC TO MS-DOS

When you are finished working with QBasic, you can return
to MS-DOS by selecting the Exit command from the File
menu. QBasic keeps track of all the changes that you make
to a file. If you attempt to exit QBasic without saving a new
program or an existing program's new contents or if you try
to open an existing file without saving the current changes,
QBasic displays a dialog box asking if you want to save the
program with the changes. If you choose not to save an existing file, the changes are lost; if you choose not to save a new
file, the entire program is lost.

PRINTING A QBASIC PROGRAM

As a program gets large, you will want to print it so that you
can view its contents easily and have a hard-copy backup.
To print a program, select the Print command from the File
menu. QBasic displays a dialog box that lets you specify
how much of the program you want to print. The Selected
Text Only option directs QBasic to print only those lines of
text that you have selected; the Current Window option directs QBasic to print only those statements that appear in the

current Program window; the Entire Program option directs QBasic to print every statement in the program. QBasic does not automatically send a formfeed to eject a page from the printer each time you print a program; consequently, you can print on the same page until it is full.

Select the appropriate option and press Enter or click on the option and then on OK with your mouse.

USING QBASIC'S BUILT-IN HELP FACILITY

QBasic provides a built-in help facility that can answer many questions. You can even use the Print command from the File menu to print the contents of any help screen, just as you would print a QBasic program by selecting text and printing it using the Selected Text Only option from the Print menu.

Press the Shift-F1 key combination to display the help screen, which explains some of the ways that you can access QBasic's help. The Contents and Index options are the keys to the information you need.

If you select the Contents option, QBasic displays the following screen:

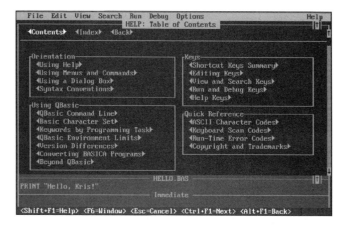

The table of contents lists topics under four subheadings. When you select a topic, a screenful of information about it appears. Triangular brackets set off any word or phase for which more information is available. Simply use the Tab key to move the cursor to the item, and press Enter.

If you select the Index option, QBasic displays the following screen:

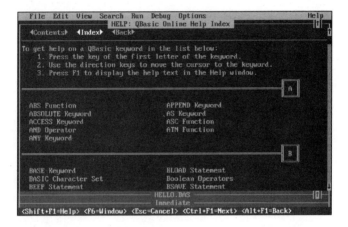

Using the direction keys, you can scroll through the index's alphabetic listing of available topics. If you want information about a topic that begins with a letter near the end of the alphabet, type in the letter, and QBasic advances to that location. If you are using a mouse, you can use the scroll bar at the right edge of the window to traverse the topics. Either way, move the cursor to the appropriate statement, and press Enter.

QBasic's help provides another option that allows you to review quickly the help text you have already accessed. The Back option directs QBasic to back up one screen at a time through a maximum of 20 previously viewed screens.

USING QBASIC'S WINDOWS

QBasic supports three different windows: the Program window, the Help window, and the Immediate window. You have already used the Program and Help windows. You typically use the Immediate window, near the bottom of the screen, to evaluate expressions when you are writing or debugging a QBasic program. The window lets you type in one statement at a time and immediately view the result. For example, assume you need to know how many hours there are in a year. Press the F6 key to move to the Immediate window or click in the window with your mouse. Then type in the following:

```
PRINT 24 * 365
```

When you press Enter, QBasic immediately displays the result (8760). Press F6 again to return to the Program window.

TRAVERSING A LONG PROGRAM FILE

As QBasic programs become more advanced, they grow much larger. QBasic provides several ways for you to move through a program file quickly. So that you have a large file to work with, open the program CATAPULT.BAS provided with QBasic in the MS-DOS directory. You could, of course, use the direction keys or the scroll bar at the right of the window to move through the text. But using the commands in the Search menu allows you to advance rapidly to a specific word or phrase.

Open the Search menu, and choose the Find command. QBasic displays a dialog box that prompts you to type in the word or phrase that you want to locate. You can also check a Match Upper/Lowercase box to direct QBasic to locate only exact matches of the word you enter and a Whole Word box if you want QBasic to locate only those matches that are surrounded by spaces or special characters. To select a box, click on it with your mouse or press the Tab key to advance the cursor to the box, and then press the Spacebar. QBasic displays an X within the box. To remove an X with the keyboard, simply move the cursor to the box and press the Spacebar again.

If the word you have chosen does not exist in the program, QBasic displays a dialog box telling you so. If the search operation locates the correct word but not the occurrence you want, repeat the search by selecting the Repeat Last Find command from the Search menu or by pressing the F3 function key.

VIEWING TWO PARTS OF A PROGRAM AT ONCE

Often you need to look at different sections of a program at the same time to see how they interrelate. With a long program, one solution is to print a hard copy. Another is to open a second window using the Split command from the View menu. The following example shows the screen split into two windows to show two sections of the program CATAPULT.BAS:

After you move to a window, you can scroll through its contents as discussed earlier. By pressing F6, you can move from one window to the next. When you are finished, select the Split command again; QBasic reverts to a single program window.

WORKING WITH QBASIC SUBPROGRAMS AND FUNCTIONS

As programs become large and more complex, programmers commonly divide them into smaller, more manageable pieces called subprograms and functions. To reduce the number of statements in the Program window that you must traverse as you program, QBasic presents each subprogram and function separately. As you work, you can edit or view only one subprogram or function at a time. The SUBs command from the View menu lets you select a specific subprogram or function for editing, viewing, or printing. In the case of CATAPULT.BAS, QBasic displays the following dialog box when you select the SUBs command:

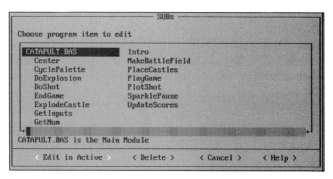

Using a mouse, you can double-click on the name of the subprogram or function you want. Or you can highlight the subprogram or function name using the direction keys, and press Enter. If you decide not to select a subprogram or function, simply press Esc to close the dialog box and return to the Program window.

CUTTING, COPYING, AND PASTING TEXT

You will do much of your editing by moving the cursor and
then adding or deleting statements. However, you can also
use the commands in QBasic's Edit menu to copy, move, or
even delete several lines of a program at one time.

Start a new program, and type in the following:

```
PRINT "This is line 3"
PRINT "This is line 4"
PRINT "Delete this line"
PRINT "This is line 1"
PRINT "This is line 2"
PRINT "Delete me, too"
```

As you can see, some of the lines are out of order, and two
need to be deleted. First select the first two program lines. If
you're using the keyboard, place the cursor at the beginning
of the first line, hold down the Shift key, and press the Down
direction key twice; if you're using a mouse, place the cursor
at the start of the first line, hold down the mouse's left button, and move the pointer down. Next open the Edit menu,
and choose the Cut command to delete the lines. Then move
the cursor to the beginning of the line that immediately follows the PRINT statement for line 2, open the Edit menu
again, and choose the Paste command. QBasic inserts the
two lines just deleted in the new location. Next delete the
two unwanted statements by selecting each statement and
choosing the Cut command from the Edit menu.

When you cut text, QBasic removes it from the program and
places it onto a clipboard that resides in your computer's
memory. When you choose the Copy command from the
Edit menu, QBasic copies the selected text onto the clipboard but does not remove the text from the program, as it
does when it performs a Cut operation. When you perform a
Paste operation, QBasic copies the clipboard's contents to
the specified location. When you perform a second Cut or
Copy operation, QBasic overwrites the clipboard's contents
with the new text. The Clear command from the Edit menu

deletes the selected text and does not copy it to the clipboard. After you choose Clear, you cannot restore the deleted text.

FINDING AND REPLACING A WORD OR PHRASE

Manually changing each instance of a specific word or phrase in a long program can be time consuming. The Change command from the Search menu, however, makes it easy to replace one word or phrase with another. In the program you just corrected, for example, you can use the Change command to alter one or more occurrences of the words *This is* to *Output for*.

To begin, open the Search menu, and choose the Change command. QBasic displays the following dialog box:

```
┌─────────────────────────────────────────────────────────┐
│                                                          │
│  Find What: ┌──────────────────────────────────────────┐ │
│             └──────────────────────────────────────────┘ │
│                                                          │
│  Change To: ┌──────────────────────────────────────────┐ │
│             └──────────────────────────────────────────┘ │
│                                                          │
│      [ ] Match Upper/Lowercase       [ ] Whole Word      │
│                                                          │
│ < Find and Verify >  < Change All >  < Cancel >  < Help > │
└─────────────────────────────────────────────────────────┘
```

At the Find What prompt, type in *This is*. Next, press the Tab key (don't press Enter) to advance to the Change To prompt, and type in *Output for*.

As in the Find command, selecting the Match Upper/Lowercase box directs QBasic to look only for words that match exactly in case. Likewise, selecting the Whole Word box directs QBasic to match only those occurrences that are surrounded by spaces or special characters. Choosing the Find and Verify option directs QBasic to locate each match and then prompt you to indicate whether you want to change that

specific occurrence. Choosing the Change All option directs
QBasic to change each occurrence automatically without
prompting you to verify that you want the change. Choosing
the Cancel option aborts the search-and-replace operation.
Pressing Enter after responding to the Change To prompt
selects the default Find and Verify option.

For this exercise, select the default option by pressing Enter.
QBasic locates the first occurrence of the words *This is* and
then displays the following dialog box:

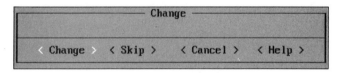

If you select the Change option, QBasic replaces the text. If
you select the Skip option, QBasic leaves the text in place
and continues its search. Choosing the Cancel option will
end the search-and-replace operation.

DEBUGGING A QBASIC PROGRAM

Debugging is the process of removing errors from a program. QBasic helps you locate two types: syntax errors and
logic errors. A syntax error typically is a keystroke error,
such as the omission of the double quotation mark from the
end of a character string. When QBasic encounters a syntax
error, it displays a dialog box containing an error message.

To help you reduce the number of syntax errors in a program, QBasic supports a statement-by-statement syntax-
checking mode that can be turned on and off with the
Syntax Checking command in the Options menu. By default,
syntax checking is enabled. You should leave it enabled in
order to identify errors as quickly as possible.

When a program runs but does not run correctly, it contains
at least one logic error. Logic errors are more difficult to de-
tect than syntax errors. In the past, programmers placed
PRINT statements throughout their programs to provide

clues as to where logic errors resided. QBasic provides a
powerful collection of debugging aids that will help you find
logic errors without using PRINT statements.

To begin, start a new program, and type in the following:

```
i = 0
increment = 1
WHILE i < 10
        PRINT i
        i = increment
WEND
```

The program's purpose is to display the numbers 0 through
9. However, when you run the program, it enters an infinite
loop, displaying the value 1 over and over. To interrupt the
program, press the Ctrl-Break key combination. Then open
the Debug menu. QBasic displays the following:

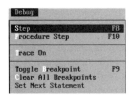

The Step command lets you execute the program one statement at a time, giving you a chance to view the output
screen or to display a variable's value at different times in
the Immediate window.

The Procedure Step command lets you execute in one step a
procedure that you know to be correct. When you have divided a program into several subprograms and functions,
this option will save you a great deal of time.

Choosing the Trace On command directs QBasic to highlight
each statement as the program executes. By observing the
highlighted statements, you can check whether the program
executes statements in the order that you anticipate.

The Toggle Breakpoint command lets you enable and disable breakpoints, which are locations at which you can suspend program execution. By setting breakpoints throughout

a program (there is no limit to the number you can set), you can stop execution immediately before locations that you suspect contain errors so that you can step through the statements one at a time. To set a breakpoint, move the cursor to the line containing the statement at which you want to suspend execution, and set a breakpoint by pressing the F9 key. To remove the breakpoint, place the cursor on the same line, and press F9 again.

Choosing the Clear All Breakpoints command removes all breakpoints from the program.

Lastly, the Set Next Statement command lets you alter the program's normal sequence of execution by directing QBasic to resume execution at whatever statement is on the same line as the cursor. By changing the execution flow, you can bypass a working section of code to continue debugging at a specific location.

In addition, QBasic's Run menu has three commands closely related to debugging: Start, Restart, and Continue. Choosing the Start command directs QBasic to run the program, starting it at the first executable statement. Choosing the Restart command directs QBasic to clear any data that was entered while the program ran and highlight the first executable statement without executing the program. The Continue command lets you resume normal execution from the current statement. This command is convenient when you are ready to continue normal execution after having suspended the program with a breakpoint.

For this exercise, choose the Trace On command, and then execute the program again by pressing the Shift-F5 key combination. As the program runs, QBasic will toggle between the output and environment screens, highlighting each statement as it executes. In this case, it is easy to see that the program is stuck in the WHILE/WEND loop. As before, use Ctrl-Break to interrupt the program. Then use the Step command (or the F8 key) to step through the program's statements. Each time a statement completes, you can press the F4 key to view the output screen or press F6 to move to the

Immediate window so that you can execute PRINT statements to check the values of the variables. It won't take you long to figure out that the value of variable i is not being incremented but rather repeatedly being assigned the value of *increment*. Thus, if you change the statement $i = increment$ to $i = i + increment$, the program will run correctly.

Admittedly, the program in this exercise is so short that you could have quickly found the error on your own. However, in more complex programs, QBasic's debugging tools will be quite an asset.

QBasic Statements and Functions

ABS Function

Returns the absolute value of a numeric expression.

Syntax:

ABS(*numeric_expression*)

Notes:

- *numeric_expression* is any numeric expression.

- ABS always returns a positive value, regardless of whether the result of the expression is positive or negative.

- ABS returns a value of the same type as *numeric_expression* (integer, long integer, double-precision, and so on).

Example:

```
PRINT "Absolute value of -3 * 5 is"; ABS(-3 * 5)
PRINT "Absolute value of 3 * 5 is"; ABS(3 * 5)
```

Running this program produces the following display:

```
Absolute value of -3 * 5 is 15
Absolute value of 3 * 5 is 15
```

ASC Function

Returns the numeric ASCII code value for the first character in a string expression.

Syntax:

ASC(*string_expression*)

Notes:

■ *string_expression* is any string expression.

Example:

```
stringvar$ = "ABC"
PRINT ASC(stringvar$)
PRINT ASC("abc")
```

Running this program produces the following display:

```
65
97
```

Related functions: CHR$

ATN Function

Returns the arctangent of the specified value.

Syntax:

ATN(*numeric_expression*)

Notes:

■ *numeric_expression* is the value for which you want to find the arctangent.

■ You can express an angle in either degrees or radians. ATN returns an angle in radians. To convert radians to degrees, use the following equation:

degrees = *radians* $*$ (180 / 3.141593)

Example:

```
value = TAN(.7854)    'Tangent of pi/4
PRINT "Arctangent is"; ATN(value)
```

Running this program produces the following display:

```
Arctangent is .7854
```

Related functions: COS; SIN; TAN

BEEP Statement

Sounds the computer's built-in speaker.

Syntax:

BEEP

Notes:

- BEEP sounds a brief tone that is useful in getting the user's attention. BEEP does not affect the screen display.

Example:

```
BEEP
PRINT "Error accessing file SALES.DAT"
```

Running this program produces the following display:

(Tone from speaker)

```
Error accessing file SALES.DAT
```

Related functions: PLAY

Related statements: PLAY; SOUND

BLOAD Statement

Loads a memory-image file created by the BSAVE statement into memory at the specified location.

Syntax:

BLOAD *filename*[, *offset*]

Notes:

■ *filename* is a string expression that specifies the file containing the image to load.

■ *offset* is the optional offset from the start of the data segment (or last DEF SEG), indicating where the image is to be loaded.

■ BLOAD and BSAVE work together to provide you with a quick and convenient way to load array values or graphics images.

■ Do not use BLOAD with files created by BASICA. QBasic and BASICA store items differently in memory.

Example:

```
'Create an array called SALES
DIM sales (1 TO 500)

'Set the segment address to the start of SALES
DEF SEG = VARSEG(sales(1))

'Load the array using BLOAD
BLOAD "SALES.DAT", VARPTR(sales(1))

'Return to the Basic data segment
DEF SEG
```

Related functions: VARPTR; VARSEG

Related statements: BSAVE; DEF SEG

BSAVE Statement

Copies the contents of a memory region to an output file or device.

Syntax:

BSAVE *filename, offset, length*

Notes:

- *filename* is a string expression that specifies the file or device to which memory contents will be transferred.

- *offset* is the location within the current segment of the first byte you want to copy.

- *length* is the number of bytes to copy (from 0 through 65,535).

- BSAVE performs a byte-by-byte copy. If you save the memory contents to a file, you can later use BLOAD to restore the memory image.

Example:

```
'Create an array with 500 elements
'Initialize the array with values from 1 through 500
DIM sales(1 TO 500)
FOR i = 1 TO 500
    sales(i) = i
NEXT i

'Set the segment address to the start of sales
DEF SEG = VARSEG(sales(1))

'Save the array using BSAVE
BSAVE "SALES.DAT", VARPTR(sales(1)), 2000

'Return to the Basic data segment
DEF SEG
```

Related functions: VARPTR; VARSEG

Related statements: BLOAD; DEF SEG

CALL Statement

Transfers control to a Basic subprogram.

Syntax:

CALL *subprogram_name* [(*argument_list*)]

or

subprogram_name [*argument_list*]

Notes:

■ *subprogram_name* is the name of a Basic subprogram created using a SUB statement.

■ *argument_list* is a list of parameters separated by commas. The subprogram can change the values of the parameters.

■ You can call subprograms with or without the CALL keyword. If you omit CALL, do not place the arguments within parentheses. Also, if you omit CALL, you must use the DECLARE statement. If you omit a declaration, QBasic will supply it automatically.

■ To prevent a subprogram from changing a parameter's value, simply place the parameter within parentheses:

```
CALL TEST (a, b, (c))
```

■ In this case, the subprogram can change the values of the parameters *a* and *b*, but not *c*.

Example:

```
DECLARE SUB SwapVal (a, b)
a = 1
b = 2
CALL SwapVal(a, b)
PRINT a; b
END

SUB SwapVal(x, y)
temp = x
x = y
y = temp
END SUB
```

Running this program produces the following display:

```
2 1
```

Related statements: CALL ABSOLUTE; CHAIN; DECLARE

CALL ABSOLUTE Statement

Transfers control to a machine-language subroutine.

Syntax:

CALL ABSOLUTE ([*parameter_list*,] *offset*)

Notes:

- *parameter_list* is an optional list of parameters separated by commas.

- *offset* is the location within the current code segment of the start of the procedure.

Example:

```
'Create a machine-language procedure and
'call it using CALL ABSOLUTE

'Array to store machine code
DIM asmroutine(1 TO 6) AS INTEGER

'Data that makes up machine-code routine
DATA &H55             : ' PUSH BP
DATA &H8B, &HEC       : ' MOV BP, SP
DATA &HB4, 2          : ' MOV AH, 2
DATA &HB2, 65         : ' MOV DL, 65
DATA &HCD, &H21       : ' INT 21H
DATA &H5D             : ' POP BP
DATA &HCB, 0          : ' RET

'Get array offset
offset = VARPTR(asmroutine(1))

'Change the segment to the start of the array
DEF SEG = VARSEG(asmroutine(1))

'Fill the array with machine code
FOR i = 0 TO 11
    READ asmcode
    POKE (offset + i), asmcode
NEXT i
```

```
'Call the routine and restore the segment
CALL ABSOLUTE(VARPTR(asmroutine(1)))
DEF SEG
```

Related statements: CALL

CDBL Function

Converts a numeric expression to a double-precision value.

Syntax:

CDBL(*numeric_expression*)

Notes:

■ *numeric_expression* is any numeric expression.

■ Using CDBL is equivalent to assigning the expression to a double-precision variable.

■ Single-precision values have 7 significant digits. Double-precision values have 15 significant digits.

Example:

```
PRINT 5 / 6
PRINT CDBL(5 / 6)
```

Running this program produces the following display:

```
.8333333
.8333333333333334
```

Related functions: CINT; CLNG; CSNG

CHAIN Statement

Transfers control from one QBasic program to another.

Syntax:

CHAIN *filename*

Notes:

- *filename* is a character string containing the filename of the program to which control is to be passed.

- To exchange information between chained programs, you must use the COMMON statement.

- After you transfer control to another program using CHAIN, the program that called CHAIN does not resume control when the chained program completes.

Example:

```
CHAIN "TEST.BAS"
```

Related statements: CALL; COMMON; RUN

CHDIR Statement

Changes the default directory for the specified drive.

Syntax:

CHDIR *directory_name*

Notes:

- *directory_name* is a string expression containing the desired directory name. It must have fewer than 64 characters.

- To change the default directory for a drive other than the current drive, precede the pathname with a disk drive letter and a colon.

- CHDIR does not change the default drive.

- You cannot abbreviate CHDIR.

Example:

```
'Change the current directory in
'drive C to \DOS
CHDIR "C:\DOS"
```

Related statements: FILES; MKDIR; RMDIR

CHR$ Function

Returns a one-character string containing the character that corresponds to the specified ASCII value.

Syntax:

CHR$(*ascii_value*)

Notes:

- *ascii_value* is the ASCII code of the desired character.

- CHR$ is commonly used to sound the computer bell (CHR$(7)).

- The standard ASCII values range from 0 through 127. The IBM PC and compatibles support extended ASCII characters from 128 through 255. Many extended characters are useful for drawing boxes and other simple graphics.

Example:

```
'Display the ASCII and extended ASCII character sets

FOR i = 0 TO 255
    PRINT i; CHR$(i)
NEXT i
```

Related functions: ASC

CINT Function

Rounds a numeric expression to an integer value.

Syntax:

CINT(*numeric_expression*)

Notes:

- *numeric_expression* must result in a value in the range −32,768 through 32,767. If the expression is outside this range, a runtime error occurs.

- CINT rounds; it does not truncate.

Example:

```
PRINT CINT(34.51)
PRINT CINT(34.49)
```

Running this program produces the following display:

```
35
34
```

Related functions: CDBL; CLNG; CSNG

CIRCLE Statement

Draws a circle or ellipse with the specified radius and center.

Syntax:

CIRCLE [**STEP**] (*x, y*), *radius* [, [*color*][, [*start_angle*] [, [*end_angle*][, *aspect_ratio*]]]]

Notes:

- STEP is an optional keyword that tells CIRCLE that the *x* and *y* values are offsets from the current graphics cursor position.

- *x, y* are the coordinates of the circle's center.

- *radius* is the radius of the circle in the current coordinate system.

- *color* is the border color for the circle. The circle is not filled.

- *start_angle* is the starting angle in radians for the arc. The default is 0.

- *end_angle* is the ending angle in radians for the arc. The default is 2π.

- *aspect_ratio* is the ratio of the length of the *y* axis to the length of the *x* axis. By changing the aspect ratio, you can create ellipses.

Example:

```
'Fill the screen with random circles
SCREEN 1
FOR i = 1 TO 100
     x = INT(320 * RND)
     y = INT(200 * RND)
     RADIUS = INT(100 * RND)
     CIRCLE (x, y), RADIUS
NEXT i
SCREEN 0
```

Related functions: POINT

Related statements: COLOR; DRAW; LINE; PAINT; PRESET; PSET; SCREEN

CLEAR Statement

Initializes all program variables, closes all files, and optionally defines the stack size.

Syntax:

CLEAR [, , *stack_size*]

Notes:

■ CLEAR closes all open files, sets all numeric variables and arrays to 0, and sets all string variables to zero length.

■ If your program uses recursion or performs several levels of subroutine calls, you might need to increase your program's stack size.

■ *stack_size* is the size of the stack in bytes. You must precede the stack size with two commas as shown.

■ The default stack size is 2048 bytes.

■ Do not execute CLEAR within a subroutine.

Example:

```
'Initialize variables and create a stack of 4096 bytes
CLEAR , , 4096
```

Related functions: FRE

Related statements: ERASE

CLNG Function

Rounds a numeric expression to a long (4-byte) integer.

Syntax:

CLNG(*numeric_expression*)

Notes:

■ *numeric_expression* must evaluate to a value in the range −2,147,483,648 through 2,147,483,647. If the result is outside this range, a runtime error occurs.

Example:

```
PRINT CLNG(338457.8)
PRINT CLNG(2147358.28)
```

Running this program produces the following display:

```
338458
2147358
```

Related functions: CDBL; CINT; CSNG

CLOSE Statement

Closes one or more files or devices opened by the OPEN statement.

Syntax:

CLOSE [[#]*file_number* [, [#]*file_number*]]...

Notes:

■ *file_number* is the file number assigned to the file or device in its OPEN statement.

■ You can specify more than one file number in a single CLOSE statement.

■ Once you close a file number, you cannot use the file number for read or write operations until you open a new file.

■ The CLEAR, END, RESET, RUN, and SYSTEM statements close your files automatically. For housekeeping purposes, however, you should issue a corresponding CLOSE statement for each OPEN statement in your program.

■ CLOSE with no arguments closes all open files and devices.

Example:

```
OPEN "TEST.DAT" FOR OUTPUT AS #1
PRINT #1, "This is a test"
CLOSE #1
```

Related statements: OPEN; RESET

CLS Statement

Clears the screen display.

Syntax:

CLS [{0 | 1 | 2}]

Notes:

■ Depending on the region of the screen that you want to clear, CLS gives you four options:

Statement	Result
CLS	Clears text or graphics viewport
CLS 0	Clears entire screen of text and graphics
CLS 1	Clears only the graphics viewport
CLS 2	Clears only the text viewport, leaving the bottom line unchanged

Example:

CLS

Related statements: VIEW; VIEW PRINT; WINDOW

COLOR Statement

Sets the screen color.

Syntax:

COLOR [*foreground*][, [*background*][, *border*]]
    (Screen mode 0)

COLOR [*background*][, *palette*]
    (Screen mode 1)

COLOR [*foreground*][, *background*]
    (Screen modes 7–10)

COLOR [*foreground*]
    (Screen modes 4, 12, 13)

Notes:

■ The COLOR statement allows you to set text foreground and background colors as well as color palettes in graphics mode.

■ See the SCREEN statement for specifics on each screen mode.

■ In screen mode 0, you can set the text foreground color to one of 16 colors (0 through 15). To use the blinking version of the color, add the value 16 to the color, yielding a value in the range 16 through 31. The background screen border must be a color value from 0 through 15.

■ In screen mode 1, you can specify a palette value in the range 0 through 255. The palette determines which of two sets of colors to use for graphics display.

■ In screen modes 7 through 10, the foreground color is an attribute number and the background color is a color number.

■ In screen modes 4, 12, and 13, the foreground color is an attribute number. You cannot specify a background color.

Example:

```
SCREEN 0
FOR fcolor = 0 TO 31
     COLOR fcolor
     PRINT "Current color is"; fcolor
     INPUT dummy$
NEXT fcolor
```

Related functions: POINT; SCREEN

Related statements: CIRCLE; DRAW; LINE; PAINT; PALETTE; PALETTE USING; PRESET; PSET; SCREEN

COM Statement

Enables or disables data communications event trapping on the specified port.

Syntax:

COM(*n*) **ON**

or

COM(*n*) **OFF**

or

COM(*n*) **STOP**

Notes:

■ *n* is the number of the communications port (1 or 2).

■ COM ON enables communications event trapping. If a character arrives at the port, your program will execute the subroutine defined by the ON COM statement.

■ COM OFF disables communications event trapping. Characters arriving at the port are ignored.

■ COM STOP prevents event trapping until the program executes a COM ON statement. Events are processed once trapping is enabled.

Example:

```
ON COM(1) GOSUB ComHandler
COM(1) ON
```

Related statements: ON *event* GOSUB

COMMON Statement

Defines variables as global within a module or between chained programs.

Syntax:

COMMON [SHARED] *variable_list*

Notes:

■ The SHARED keyword states that the specified variables are shared by all subprograms and functions in a module.

■ *variable_list* is the list of global variables with variable names separated by commas. QBasic allows you to specify variables as

variable_name[()] [**AS** *type*]

■ COMMON statements must appear before any executable statements in your program. QBasic associates variables in common blocks by position, not by name.

Example:

```
COMMON a, b, c
a = 1: b = 2: c = 3
CHAIN "COMMON.BAS"

'Code for COMMON.BAS
COMMON x, y, z
PRINT x, y, z
```

Running this program produces the following display:

```
1       2       3
```

Related statements: STATIC

CONST Statement

Defines a symbolic constant.

Syntax:

CONST *symbol_name* = *expression* [, *symbol_name* = *expression*]...

Notes:

■ Constants allow your programs to use symbolic names in place of numeric or string values.

■ *symbol_name* is the name that the constant will have throughout your program. You cannot change the value of a constant once you have defined it.

■ *expression* is a numeric or string expression assigned to the constant. You cannot use variables or functions in the expression.

■ Constants defined in a subprogram or function are local to that subprogram or function.

Example:

```
CONST true = 1
CONST daysperweek = 7

'Use constant in array declaration
DIM Days(daysperweek)
```

COS Function

Returns the cosine of the specified angle.

Syntax:

COS(*angle*)

Notes:

■ *angle* is a numeric expression that specifies an angle in radians.

■ You can express an angle in radians or degrees. The QBasic trigonometric routines support only radians.
To convert from degrees to radians, use the following equation:

radians = 3.141593 $*$ (*degrees* / 180)

Example:

```
angle = .785
PRINT "Cosine of"; angle; "is"; COS(angle)
```

Running this program produces the following display:

```
Cosine of .785 is .7073882
```

Related functions: ATN; SIN; TAN

CSNG Function

Converts a numeric expression to a single-precision value.

Syntax:

CSNG(*numeric_expression*)

Notes:

■ *numeric_expression* is any numeric expression.

■ Using CSNG is equivalent to assigning the expression to a single-precision variable.

■ Single-precision values have seven significant digits.

Example:

```
a# = 6
b# = 7
PRINT a#/b#, CSNG(a#/b#)
```

Running this program produces the following display:

```
 .8571428571428571          .8571429
```

Related functions: CDBL; CINT; CLNG

CSRLIN Function

Returns the current cursor row number.

Syntax:

CSRLIN

Notes:

■ CSRLIN returns the cursor's line (row) number. POS returns the cursor's column number.

Example:

```
'Save cursor row and column
saveline = CSRLIN
savecol = POS(0)
'Move to line 10, column 20
LOCATE 10,20: PRINT "Message at 10,20"
'Restore cursor to previous position
LOCATE saveline, savecol
```

Related functions: POS

Related statements: LOCATE

CVD Function

Converts an 8-byte string (created by MKD$) to a double-precision value.

Syntax:

CVD(*eight_byte_string*)

Example:

```
OPEN "PAYROLL.DAT" FOR RANDOM AS #3 LEN = 35
FIELD #3, 27 AS names$, 8 AS salary$
GET #3, 1
PRINT "EMPLOYEE: "; name$
PRINT "Salary $"; CVD(salary$)
CLOSE #3
```

Related functions: CVDMBF; CVI; CVL; CVS; CVSMBF; MKD$; MKDMBF$; MKI$; MKL$; MKS$; MKSMBF$

CVDMBF Function

Converts an 8-byte string containing a double-precision
value (created by MKDMBF$) from Microsoft binary format
to IEEE format.

Syntax:

CVDMBF(*eight_byte_string*)

Notes:

■ CVDMBF, CVSMBF, MKDMBF$, and MKSMBF$ are
  useful for maintaining data files created with earlier versions of Basic.

Example:

See CVD

Related functions: CVD; CVI; CVL; CVS; CVSMBF;
MKD$; MKDMBF$; MKI$; MKL$; MKS$; MKSMBF$

CVI Function

Converts a 2-byte string (created by MKI$) to an integer
value.

Syntax:

CVI(*two_byte_string*)

Example:

See CVD

Related functions: CVD; CVDMBF; CVL; CVS; CVSMBF;
MKD$; MKDMBF$; MKI$; MKL$; MKS$; MKSMBF$

CVL Function

Converts a 4-byte string (created by MKL$) to a long integer value.

Syntax:

CVL(*four_byte_string*)

Example:

See CVD

Related functions: CVD; CVDMBF; CVI; CVS; CVSMBF; MKD$; MKDMBF$; MKI$; MKL$; MKS$; MKSMBF$

CVS Function

Converts a 4-byte string (created by MKS$) to a single-precision value.

Syntax:

CVS(*four_byte_string*)

Example:

See CVD

Related functions: CVD; CVDMBF; CVI; CVL; CVSMBF; MKD$; MKDMBF$; MKI$; MKL$; MKS$; MKSMBF$

CVSMBF Function

Converts a 4-byte string containing a single-precision value (created by MKSMBF$) from Microsoft binary format to IEEE format.

Syntax:

CVSMBF(*four_byte_string*)

Notes:

■ CVDMBF, CVSMBF, MKDMBF$, and MKSMBF$ are useful for maintaining data files created with earlier versions of Basic.

Example:

See CVD

Related functions: CVD; CVDMBF; CVI; CVL; CVS; MKD$; MKDMBF$; MKI$; MKL$; MKS$; MKSMBF$

DATA Statement

Stores numeric and string constants to be read with the READ statement.

Syntax:

DATA *constant* [, *constant*]...

Notes:

■ *constant* is a numeric or string constant.

■ READ statements access DATA statements in the order the DATA statements appear in your program. The RESTORE statement allows your program to reread DATA statements as necessary.

■ The type of a variable in a READ statement must match the type of the constant in the DATA statement.

■ You can only use data statements at the module level, never in a procedure.

Example:

```
DATA 1, 2.2345, "TEST", 98765
READ a%, b#, c$, d$
PRINT a%, b#, c$, d$
```

Running this program produces the following display:

```
1       2.2345      TEST       98765
```

Related statements: READ; RESTORE

DATE$ Function

Returns a 10-character string containing the current system date in the form *mm-dd-yyyy*.

Syntax:

DATE$

Example:

```
PRINT DATE$
```

Running this program line on January 13, 1991, produces the following display:

```
01-13-1991
```

Related statements: DATE$; TIME$

DATE$ Statement

Sets the system date.

Syntax:

DATE$ = *string_expression*

Notes:

- *string_expression* is a string expression containing the desired date in the form "*mm-dd-yyyy*" where *mm* is the month (1 through 12), *dd* is the day (1 through 31), and *yyyy* is the year (1980 through 2099).

- If you specify only the last two digits of the year, DATE$ assumes that the first two digits are 19.

- DATE$ allows you to use either dashes or slashes to separate the date fields.

Example:

```
DATE$ = "12/25/89"
```

Related functions: DATE$; TIME$

DECLARE Statement

Declares a procedure and directs QBasic to perform type checking for each parameter.

Syntax:

DECLARE {**FUNCTION** | **SUB**} *procedure_name*
  [([*argument_list*])]

Notes:

- DECLARE directs QBasic to ensure that the types of parameters passed to a procedure match the types that the procedure expects.

- DECLARE is needed only when you don't use the CALL keyword.

- The keyword FUNCTION indicates that the procedure is a function; likewise, SUB indicates a subprogram.

- *procedure_name* is the name of the function or subprogram.

■ *argument_list* is an optional list of parameters separated by commas. For compiler type checking, specify arguments as follows:

variable_name [**AS** *type*]

■ Valid types include INTEGER, LONG, SINGLE, DOUBLE, STRING, ANY, or a user-defined type. ANY allows any type for that parameter.

Example:
See CALL

Related statements: CALL; FUNCTION; SUB

DEF FN Statement

Defines a function.

Syntax:
DEF FN*name* [(*argument_list*)] = *expression*

or

DEF FN*name* [(*argument_list*)]
    ⋮
FN*name* = *expression*
    ⋮
END DEF

Notes:
■ Function names must begin with FN and can contain up to 40 characters. The function name indicates the value type the function returns:

Function Name	Returns
FNday$	string
FNcount%	integer
FNaverage#	single-precision value

- For a function to return a value, the function must assign its result to the function name.

- *argument_list* is a list of parameters to the function separated by commas as follows:

  argument_name [**AS** *type*]

- You cannot use a function before your program defines it, nor can you use DEF FN functions recursively.

Example:

```
DEF FNsum (a AS INTEGER, b AS INTEGER) = a + b

DEF FNmax (a AS INTEGER, b AS INTEGER, c AS INTEGER)
    IF (a > b) THEN
        max = a
    ELSE
        max = b
    END IF
    IF (max > c) THEN
        FNmax = max
    ELSE
        FNmax = c
    END IF
END DEF

PRINT FNsum(3, 5)
PRINT FNmax(1, 2, 3)
```

Running this program produces the following display:

```
8
3
```

Related statements: EXIT; FUNCTION

DEF SEG Statement

Sets the current segment address for subsequent PEEK functions and BLOAD, BSAVE, CALL ABSOLUTE, and POKE statements.

Syntax:

DEF SEG [= *address*]

Notes:

■ *address* is an integer expression in the range 0 through 65,535. If you omit *address*, QBasic uses the Basic data segment.

Example:

See CALL ABSOLUTE statement

Related functions: PEEK

Related statements: BLOAD; BSAVE; CALL ABSOLUTE; POKE

DEFDBL Statement

Defines the default data type as double-precision for variables whose names begin with a letter in the specified range.

Syntax:

DEFDBL *letter*[- *last_letter*][, *letter*[-*last_letter*]]...

Notes:

■ *letter* and *last_letter* are a range of letters to associate with a type. QBasic does not distinguish between uppercase and lowercase variables.

■ If a variable name has the suffix %, &, !, #, or $, the data type associated with the suffix takes precedence over the default type statement.

Example:

```
DEFDBL A-J
```

Related statements: DEFINT; DEFLNG; DEFSNG; DEFSTR

DEFINT Statement

Defines the default data type as integer for variables whose
names begin with a letter in the specified range.

Syntax:

DEFINT *letter*[- *last_letter*][, *letter*[-*last_letter*]]...

Notes:

See DEFDBL

Example:

```
DEFINT X-Z
```

Related statements: DEFDBL; DEFLNG; DEFSNG;
DEFSTR

DEFLNG Statement

Defines the default data type as long for variables whose
names begin with a letter in the specified range.

Syntax:

DEFLNG *letter*[- *last_letter*][, *letter*[- *last_letter*]]...

Notes:

See DEFDBL

Example:

```
DEFLNG L-N
```

Related statements: DEFDBL; DEFINT; DEFSNG;
DEFSTR

DEFSNG Statement

Defines the default data type as single-precision for variables whose names begin with a letter in the specified range.

Syntax:

DEFSNG *letter*[- *last_letter*][, *letter*[-*last_letter*]]...

Notes:

See DEFDBL

Example:

```
DEFSNG T-W
```

Related statements: DEFDBL; DEFINT; DEFLNG; DEFSTR

DEFSTR Statement

Defines the default data type as string for variables whose names begin with a letter in the specified range.

Syntax:

DEFSTR *letter*[- *last_letter*][, *letter*[-*last_letter*]]...

Notes:

See DEFDBL

Example:

```
DEFSTR S
'sdate defaults to string
sdate = DATE$
PRINT sdate
```

Related statements: DEFDBL; DEFINT; DEFLNG; DEFSNG

DIM Statement

Declares an array variable and allocates storage.

Syntax:

DIM [**SHARED**] *variable_name*[(*subscripts*)][**AS** *type*] [, *variable_name*[(*subscripts*)][**AS** *type*]]...

Notes:

■ The SHARED keyword allows subprograms and functions to share the same variable without passing the variable as a parameter.

■ *variable_name* is the name of the array.

■ *subscripts* is the dimensions of the array. If you have not previously defined an array in a DIM statement, you can assign a value to an element that has subscript ranging from 0 to 10. You can change the lower and upper bounds as shown here:

```
DIM a(0 TO 8)     'a(0) to a(8)
DIM b(1 TO 10)    'b(1) to b(10)
```

■ If you specify only one subscript, QBasic assumes that it is the upper bound and uses 0 for the lower bound unless you include an OPTION BASE statement.

■ For multidimensional arrays, simply separate the subscripts of each array dimension with commas:

```
DIM box(3, 3)
DIM bigbox(1 TO 10, 1 TO 10)
```

■ The maximum number of array dimensions is 60.

■ Valid types include INTEGER, LONG, SINGLE, DOUBLE, STRING, and user-defined types.

Example:

```
DIM a(25 TO 100) AS INTEGER
DIM b(1 TO 10, 1 TO 5) AS DOUBLE

TYPE Schedule
     day AS STRING * 10
     hours AS INTEGER
END TYPE
DIM workday AS Schedule
```

Related functions: LBOUND; UBOUND

Related statements: ERASE; OPTION BASE; REDIM

DO UNTIL Statement

Repeats a set of instructions until a condition becomes true.

Syntax:

DO UNTIL *Boolean_expression*
   statements
LOOP

or

DO
   statements
LOOP UNTIL *Boolean_expression*

Notes:

- *Boolean_expression* is an expression that evaluates to true or false, such as I > 100.

- The first form of the statement first tests the Boolean expression. If the expression is true, QBasic skips the statements within the loop and continues execution at the first statement following the loop. If the expression is false, QBasic executes the statements within the loop until the expression is true.

■ The second form of the statement first performs the statements within the loop and then tests the Boolean expression. If the expression is false, QBasic repeats the statements in the loop. If the expression is true, QBasic continues execution at the first statement following the loop.

Example:

```
i = 0
DO
     PRINT i
     i = i + 1
LOOP UNTIL i = 100
```

Related statements: DO WHILE; EXIT; FOR; WHILE/WEND

DO WHILE Statement

Repeats a set of instructions while a condition is true.

Syntax:

DO WHILE *Boolean_expression*
    statements
LOOP

or

DO
    statements
LOOP WHILE *Boolean_expression*

Notes:

■ *Boolean_expression* is an expression that evaluates to true or false.

■ The first form of the statement first tests the Boolean expression. If the expression is true, QBasic executes the statements within the loop until the expression becomes false. Once the expression is false, the program continues execution at the first statement that follows the loop.

■ The second form of the statement first executes the statements within the loop and then tests the Boolean expression. If the expression is true, QBasic repeats the statements; otherwise, execution continues at the first statement after the loop.

Example:

```
i = 0
DO WHILE i < 100
    PRINT i
    i = i + 1
LOOP
```

Related statements: DO UNTIL; EXIT; FOR; WHILE/WEND

DRAW Statement

Draws an object specified in a string expression.

Syntax:

DRAW *string_expression*

Notes:

■ DRAW uses a string containing graphics commands to draw an object. The string can contain cursor, color, and scaling commands.

■ Cursor movement commands are as follows:

Command	Description	Command	Description
U [n]	Up n units	G [n]	Down and left n units
D [n]	Down n units	H [n]	Up and left n units
L [n]	Left n units	M [{−¦+}] x,y	Move to x,y (If you precede x,y with a minus or plus sign, movement is relative to the current position of the cursor.)
R [n]	Right n units		
E [n]	Up and right n units		
F [n]	Down and right n units		

If you omit n, the cursor moves one unit.

■ DRAW allows you to precede the cursor movement functions with B and N:

Command	Description
B	Move but do not draw points
N	Move but return to original position once drawn

■ Angle, color, and scaling commands are as follows:

Command	Description
A rotation	Set rotation angle in degrees: 0 = 0°, 1 = 90°, 2 = 180°, 3 = 270°
TA degree	Turn an angle (−360° through 360°)
C color	Set color
S n	Set scale factor for units (The default is 4, 1 pixel)
P color, border	Paint the interior of the object color; the color of the border must be border

Example:

```
'Draw a box and fill it
SCREEN 1
DRAW "C3"
DRAW "L20U20R20D20"        'draw box
DRAW "BH10"                'move into box
DRAW "P2,3"                'paint box
```

Related functions: POINT

Related statements: CIRCLE; COLOR; LINE; PAINT;
PRESET; PSET; SCREEN

END Statement

Ends a QBasic program.

Syntax:

END

Notes:

- END by itself terminates your program and closes all files.

- The END statement is also used with DEF, FUNCTION,
  IF, SELECT, SUB, and TYPE. Those forms of END are
  discussed in relation to the appropriate statements.

Example:

```
FOR i = 1 TO 10
     PRINT i
NEXT i
END
```

Related statements: DEF FN; FUNCTION; IF; SELECT
CASE; SUB; TYPE

ENVIRON Statement

Changes an existing entry or places a new entry in the MS-DOS environment.

Syntax:

ENVIRON *string_expression*

Notes:

■ The ENVIRON statement expects a string expression of the same form as the MS-DOS SET command, *entry=value*.

■ The change to the environment table is valid only for the life of the program.

■ You cannot increase the size of the MS-DOS environment in QBasic. To make space in the MS-DOS environment for use by QBasic programs, create a dummy entry with the DOS SET command. Then erase the contents of the entry in a QBasic program to make space for new or changed variables.

Example:

```
ENVIRON "PROGRAM=TEST"
PRINT ENVIRON$("PROGRAM")
```

Running this program produces the following display:

```
TEST
```

Related functions: ENVIRON$

ENVIRON$ Function

Returns an entry from the MS-DOS environment.

Syntax:

ENVIRON$(*entry_string*)

or

ENVIRON$(*n*)

Notes:

■ The MS-DOS SET command allows you to set and display environment strings from the MS-DOS prompt.

■ The first form of ENVIRON$ allows your program to access the value of an environment variable. The name of the desired environment variable is *entry_string*.

■ The second form of ENVIRON$ allows your program to access the *n*th environment string.

■ If the specified entry does not exist, ENVIRON$ returns a null string.

Example:

```
PRINT ENVIRON$("PATH")

i = 1
DO WHILE ENVIRON$(i) <> ""
    PRINT ENVIRON$(i)
    i = i + 1
LOOP
```

Related statements: ENVIRON

EOF Function

Tests for the end-of-file condition.

Syntax:

EOF(*file_number*)

Notes:

- EOF returns true if the end of the file associated with the file number specified has been reached; otherwise, EOF returns false.

- *file_number* is the number assigned to the file in its OPEN statement.

Example:

```
OPEN "\CONFIG.SYS" FOR INPUT AS #1
DO UNTIL EOF(1)
    LINE INPUT #1, fdata$
    PRINT fdata$
LOOP
CLOSE #1
```

Related functions: LOC; LOF

Related statements: CLOSE; OPEN

ERASE Statement

Reinitializes the elements of a static array or deallocates dynamic arrays.

Syntax:

ERASE *array* [, *array*]...

Notes:

- *array* is the name of the array to reinitialize or deallocate.

- For static numeric arrays, ERASE sets each element to zero. For static string arrays, ERASE sets each element to null.

- For dynamic arrays, ERASE frees the memory used by the specified arrays.

Example:

```
DIM a(100)
FOR i = 1 TO 100
    a(i) = i
NEXT i
ERASE a              'Reinitialize A
FOR i = 1 TO 100
    PRINT a(i)
NEXT i
```

Related functions: FRE

Related statements: CLEAR; DIM; REDIM

ERDEV Function

Returns an integer error code from the last device that declared an error.

Syntax:

ERDEV

Notes:

- The MS-DOS critical error handler sets the value for ERDEV. The lower byte contains the MS-DOS error code (0 through 12). The upper byte contains device attribute information.

Example:

```
ON ERROR GOTO Handler
  ⋮
Handler:
    PRINT "Error accessing device "; ERDEV$
    PRINT "Error status code "; ERDEV
    ⋮
```

Related functions: ERDEV$; ERL; ERR

Related statements: ERROR; ON ERROR GOTO; RESUME

ERDEV$ Function

Returns a character string containing the name of the device that generated a critical error.

Syntax:

ERDEV$

Notes:

■ The MS-DOS critical error handler sets the value for ERDEV$.

Example:

See ERDEV

Related functions: ERDEV; ERL; ERR

Related statements: ERROR; ON ERROR GOTO; RESUME

ERL Function

Returns the line number of the statement that caused the error or the closest line number before the error-causing statement.

Syntax:

ERL

Notes:

■ ERL returns only line numbers. It does not return line labels. If you are not using line numbers, ERL returns 0.

Example:

```
100 PRINT 1/0
1000 Handler:
1010        PRINT "Error processing at line"; ERL
1020        PRINT "Error number"; ERR
1030        RESUME
```

Running this program produces the following display:

```
Error processing at line 100
Error number 11
```

Related functions: ERDEV; ERDEV$; ERR

Related statements: ERROR; ON ERROR GOTO; RESUME

ERR Function

Returns the error code for the last error that occurred.

Syntax:

ERR

Notes:

Error Code	Description	Error Code	Description
1	NEXT without FOR	6	Overflow
2	Syntax error	7	Out of memory
3	RETURN without GOSUB	8	Label not defined
4	Out of DATA	9	Subscript out of range
5	Illegal function call	10	Duplicate definition

(continued)

Continued

Error Code	Description	Error Code	Description
11	Division by zero	50	FIELD overflow
12	Illegal in direct mode	51	Internal error
13	Type mismatch	52	Bad file name or number
14	Out of string space	53	File not found
16	String formula too complex	54	Bad file mode
		55	File already open
17	Cannot continue	56	FIELD statement active
18	Function not defined		
19	No RESUME	57	Device I/O error
20	RESUME without error	58	File already exists
		59	Bad record length
24	Device timeout	61	Disk full
25	Device fault	62	Input past end of file
26	FOR without NEXT	63	Bad record number
27	Out of paper	64	Bad file name
29	WHILE without WEND	67	Too many files
		68	Device unavailable
30	WEND without WHILE	69	Communication-buffer overflow
33	Duplicate label	70	Permission denied
35	Subprogram not defined	71	Disk not ready
37	Argument-count mismatch	72	Disk-media error
		73	Feature unavailable
38	Array not defined	74	Rename across disks
39	CASE ELSE expected	75	Path/File access error
40	Variable required	76	Path not found

Example:

See ERL

Related functions: ERDEV; ERDEV$; ERL

Related statements: ERROR; ON ERROR GOTO; RESUME

ERROR Statement

Simulates an occurrence of the error number specified.
Allows a program to define its own error codes.

Syntax:

ERROR *numeric_expression*

Notes:

- *numeric_expression* is an integer value in the range 1 through 255.

- See the ERR function for a list of predefined error status codes. To define your own error, use an undefined error value.

- The ERROR statement assigns the error value specified to ERR and passes control to the error handler.

Example:

```
ON ERROR GOTO HANDLER
'Test error handler with error 222
ERROR 222
EndTest:
END

Handler:
      PRINT "In error handler with error"; ERR
      RESUME EndTest
```

Related functions: ERDEV; ERDEV$; ERL; ERR

Related statements: ON ERROR GOTO; RESUME

EXIT Statements

Exit a DO or FOR loop, function, or subprogram.

Syntax:

EXIT DEF   Exits DEF FN function

or

EXIT DO   Exits a DO loop

or

EXIT FOR   Exits a FOR loop

or

EXIT FUNCTION   Exits a FUNCTION procedure

or

EXIT SUB   Exits a subprogram

Notes:

■ For DO and FOR loops, execution continues at the first statement following the loop.

■ For functions and subprograms, execution continues at the statement following the statement that called the function or subroutine.

Example:

```
j = 30
FOR i = 1 TO 50
    IF i = j THEN
        EXIT FOR
    END IF
NEXT i
PRINT "Ending value is"; i
```

Running this program produces the following display:

```
Ending value is 30
```

Related statements: DEF FN; DO UNTIL; DO WHILE; FOR; FUNCTION; SUB

EXP Function

Returns *e* raised to a specified power where *e* is the base of natural logarithms.

Syntax:

EXP(*numeric_expression*)

Notes:

■ *numeric_expression* specifies the power to which *e* should be raised. It must be less than or equal to 88.02969; otherwise, EXP results in an overflow error.

Example:

```
PRINT EXP(0), EXP(1)
```

Running this program produces the following display:

```
1      2.71828
```

Related functions: LOG

FIELD Statement

Allocates space for variables in a random-access file buffer.

Syntax:

FIELD [#] *file_number*, *width* **AS** *str_variable*...

Notes:

■ *file_number* is the number assigned to the file in its OPEN statement.

■ *width* is the number of characters in the field.

■ *str_variable* is the name of a string variable to be used when reading from or writing to the file.

- A variable name that appears in a FIELD statement should not appear in an INPUT statement or on the left side of an assignment operator. If it does, the variable will no longer reference the random-access file buffer.

- Using record variables is usually more convenient than using the FIELD statement.

Example:

```
OPEN "RANDOM.DAT" FOR RANDOM AS #1 LEN=80
FIELD #1, 76 AS name$, 4 AS salary$
```

Related statements: GET; LSET; OPEN; PUT; RSET

FILEATTR Function

Returns either the file mode or the MS-DOS file handle for an open file.

Syntax:

FILEATTR(*file_number, file_info*)

Notes:

- *file_number* is the file number assigned to the file in its OPEN statement.

- *file_info* dictates the information FILEATTR returns. If 1, FILEATTR returns the access mode:

Value	Mode
1	Input
2	Output
4	Random
8	Append
32	Binary

- If *file_info* is 2, FILEATTR returns the MS-DOS file handle.

Example:

```
OPEN "APPEND.DAT" FOR APPEND AS #1
OPEN "OUTPUT.DAT" FOR OUTPUT AS #2

PRINT "File 1 Mode"; FILEATTR(1, 1)
PRINT "File 1 Handle"; FILEATTR(1, 2)
PRINT "File 2 Mode"; FILEATTR(2, 1)
PRINT "File 2 Handle"; FILEATTR(2, 2)
CLOSE #1: CLOSE #2
```

Running this program produces the following display:

```
File 1 Mode 8
File 1 Handle 5
File 2 Mode 2
File 2 Handle 6
```

FILES Statement

Displays the names of files in the current or specified directory.

Syntax:

FILES [*string_expression*]

Notes:

■ *string_expression* is a string expression that contains an MS-DOS file specification of the files to display. Wild-card characters can be used.

■ If you omit a file specification, FILES displays the files in the current directory.

Example:

```
FILES                'List all files
FILES "*.BAS"        'List all .BAS files
FILES "A:"           'List all files on drive A
```

Related statements: CHDIR; KILL; NAME

FIX Function

Returns the integer portion of a floating-point expression.

Syntax:

FIX(*numeric_expression*)

Notes:

■ *numeric_expression* is any numeric expression.

Example:

```
PRINT FIX(-10.99)
PRINT FIX(-10.1)
```

Running this program produces the following display:

```
-10
-10
```

Related functions: INT

FOR Statement

Repeats a given set of instructions a specific number of times.

Syntax:

FOR *control_variable* = *start_value* **TO** *end_value* [**STEP** *increment*]
  ⋮
NEXT [*control_variable* [, *control_variable*]...]

Notes:

■ *control_variable* is the variable that FOR increments with each iteration of the loop. It controls whether or not QBasic repeats the loop.

■ *start_value* is the initial value that QBasic assigns to the control variable.

■ *end_value* is the value that the control variable must equal before the loop ends.

■ *increment* is the amount that QBasic adds to the control variable with each iteration of the loop. The increment can be a positive or negative value. If you omit *increment*, the default increment is 1.

■ The NEXT statement directs QBasic to increment the control variable and to test whether it is greater than the end value. If it is not, execution continues at the first statement within the loop; otherwise, execution continues at the first statement following NEXT.

Example:

```
FOR i = 1 TO 10
    PRINT "i ="; i
NEXT i

FOR i = 1 TO 10
    FOR j = 1 TO 10
        PRINT i; "*"; j; "="; i * j
    NEXT j
NEXT i
```

Related statements: DO UNTIL; DO WHILE; EXIT; WHILE/WEND

FRE Function

Returns the amount of available stack space, string space, or memory.

Syntax:

FRE(*numeric_expression*)

or

FRE(*string_expression*)

Notes:

■ If the argument to FRE is –1, FRE returns the size in bytes of the largest array you can create. If the argument is –2, FRE returns the available stack space. For any other numeric argument, FRE returns the amount of available string space.

■ If the argument to FRE is a string expression, FRE compacts the free string space into a single block and then returns the available string space.

Example:

```
PRINT "String space"; FRE("")
PRINT "Stack space"; FRE(-2)
PRINT "Array space"; FRE(-1)
```

Running this program produces the following display:

```
String space 48460
Stack space 784
Array space 184092
```

Related statements: CLEAR; ERASE

FREEFILE Function

Returns the next available Basic file number.

Syntax:

FREEFILE

Notes:

■ FREEFILE eliminates the need to hard-code file numbers and, accordingly, the risk of using a file number already in use.

Example:

```
filenumber = FREEFILE
OPEN "TEST.DAT" FOR OUTPUT AS filenumber
CLOSE filenumber
```

Related statements: OPEN

FUNCTION Statement

Declares a user-defined function.

Syntax:

FUNCTION *function_name* [(*arguments*)] [**STATIC**]

⋮

function_name = *expression*

⋮

END FUNCTION

Notes:

■ *function_name* is the name of the user-defined function. The name can end with a type-declaration character (%, &, !, #, or $) to indicate the type of value it returns.

■ *arguments* is an optional list of parameters, separated by commas, to be passed to the function.

■ To specify the type of each variable, use the following form:

variable[()] **AS** *type*

■ The STATIC keyword directs QBasic to save the values of the function's local variables between function calls.

■ For a function to return a value, the function must at some point assign an expression to the function name.

Example:

```
FUNCTION Min% (a AS INTEGER, b AS INTEGER)
    IF (a < b) then
        Min% = a
    ELSE
        Min% = b
    END IF
END FUNCTION

PRINT "Min of 5 and 3 is"; Min%(5, 3)
```

Related statements: DECLARE; DEF FN; EXIT; STATIC; SUB

GET Statement (File I/O)

Reads a record from a random-access or binary disk file.

Syntax:

GET [#]*file_number*[, [*record_number*][, *variable*]]

Notes:

■ *file_number* is the number assigned to the file in its OPEN statement.

■ *record_number* is the number of the record desired, from 1 through 2,147,483,647. If you omit a record number, GET reads the next record.

■ *variable* is the name of the variable into which GET enters the data. Usually a user-defined record variable is used.

Example:

```
TYPE SalaryRecord
    ename AS STRING * 20
    salary AS SINGLE
END TYPE
```

```
DIM employee AS SalaryRecord

OPEN "SALARY.DAT" FOR RANDOM AS #1 LEN = LEN(employee)
GET #1, 1, employee
PRINT employee.ename, employee.salary
CLOSE #1
```

Related functions: CVD; CVI; CVL; CVS; MKD$; MKI$; MKL$; MKS$

Related statements: FIELD; INPUT; LINE INPUT; LSET; PUT; RSET

GET Statement (Graphics)

Stores a graphics screen image in an array.

Syntax:

GET [**STEP**](*xleft*, *ytop*)-[**STEP**](*xright*, *ybottom*), *array*[(*index*)]

Notes:

■ GET stores the screen image contained in the specified rectangle.

■ The keyword STEP indicates that the coordinates are off-sets relative to the last point plotted.

■ *array* is the name of the array in which GET should store the image.

■ *index* is the array index at which storage of the graphics image begins.

■ To determine the number of bytes required, use the following formula:

$4 + INT(((xright - xleft + 1) * (bits\_per\_pixel/planes) + 7) / 8)$
$* planes * (ybottom - ytop + 1)$

■ The number of bits per pixel and the number of planes depends on the current screen:

Screen Mode	Bits per Pixel	Planes
1	2	1
2	1	1
3	1	1
4	1	1
7	1	4
8	1	4
9	1	*
10	1	2
11	1	1
12	1	4
13	8	1

*2 if 64 KB of EGA memory; otherwise 4.

Example:

```
GET (10, 20)-(20, 50), animal
```

Related statements: PUT (Graphics); SCREEN

GOSUB Statement

Directs execution to continue at a Basic subroutine.

Syntax:

GOSUB *location*

Notes:

■ *location* is either a line number or label at which execution should continue.

■ Use a RETURN statement to end a subroutine.

■ GOSUB is the older method of accessing subroutines. Most new programs use QBasic SUB and CALL statements.

Example:

```
GOSUB Test
END
Test:
      PRINT "In subroutine Test"
      RETURN
```

Related statements: ON *event* GOSUB; ON *expression*; RETURN; SUB

GOTO Statement

Branches to the specified line number or label.

Syntax:

GOTO *location*

Notes:

■ *location* is the line number or label at which execution is to continue.

■ Early versions of Basic did not have DO loops, ELSE clauses for IF statements, or SELECT CASE statements. They used GOTO to implement these constructs. To improve your programs' readability and simplify debugging, restrict the use of GOTO.

Example:

```
i = 0
Start:
      PRINT "i ="; i
      INPUT "Again"; reply$
      IF reply$="N" THEN
            END
```

```
ELSE
        i = i + 1
    END IF
GOTO Start
```

Related statements: DO UNTIL; DO WHILE; IF; SELECT CASE

HEX$ Function

Returns a character string containing the hexadecimal representation of a value.

Syntax:

HEX$(*numeric_expression*)

Notes:

■ Hexadecimal notation is the base 16 numbering system. It uses the numbers 1 through 9 and the letters A through F. To store the hexadecimal representation of a number, you must use a string variable.

Example:

```
'Display octal, decimal, and
'hex values from 0 to 255
FOR i = 0 TO 255
    PRINT OCT$(i), i, HEX$(i)
NEXT i
```

Related functions: OCT$

IF Statement

Provides conditional execution based on the evaluation of an expression.

Syntax:

IF *expression* **THEN** *true_statement* [**ELSE** *false_statement*]

or

IF *expression* **THEN**

    [*true_statements*]

[**ELSEIF** *expression* **THEN**

    [*true_statements*]]

⋮

[**ELSE**

    [*false_statements*]]

END IF

Notes:

■ The first form of the statement allows you to execute a single statement if the expression is true and a different statement if the expression is false.

■ The second form of the statement allows you to execute a series of statements if the expression is true and a different set if the expression is false. Also, this syntax allows you to test for a series of different conditions, one after another.

Example:

```
IF (a > b) THEN max = a ELSE max = b

IF (a > max) THEN CALL BigValue(a)

IF (day$ = "MONDAY") THEN
     CALL Meetings
     CALL Dinners
ELSE
     CALL Gym
END IF

IF (DAY$ = "MONDAY") THEN
     CALL Meetings
ELSEIF (DAY$ = "THURSDAY") THEN
     CALL Tickets
```

```
ELSEIF (DAY$ = "FRIDAY") THEN
    CALL Theatre
END IF
```

Related statements: ON *expression*; SELECT CASE

INKEY$ Function

Reads a character from the keyboard.

Syntax:

INKEY$

Notes:

■ INKEY$ returns a null string if no character is present, a 1-byte string for standard keys, and a 2-byte string for extended keys.

■ For extended keys, the first character is a null character (ASCII 0) and the second is the keyboard scan code.

■ INKEY$ does not echo the character to the screen.

Example:

```
PRINT "Press a series of keys - F10 to stop"
DO
    DO
        k$ = INKEY$
    LOOP WHILE k$ = ""
    IF LEN(k$) = 1 THEN
        PRINT "Letter", k$
    ELSE
        PRINT "Scan code", ASC(MID$(k$, 2, 1))
    END IF
LOOP UNTIL MID$(k$, 2, 1) = CHR$(68)        'F10 scan code
```

INP Function

Returns a byte read from an I/O port.

Syntax:

INP(*port_number*)

Notes:

■ *port_number* is the number associated with the desired
port. It must be in the range 0 through 65,535.

Example:

```
'Turn on speaker through port 97
saveval = INP(97)
OUT 97, saveval + 3
DO
LOOP WHILE INKEY$ = ""
OUT 97, saveval
```

Related statements: OUT

INPUT Statement

Gets keyboard input.

Syntax:

INPUT [;] ["*prompt*"{; | ,}] *variables*

Notes:

■ A semicolon immediately after INPUT directs QBasic to
leave the cursor on the same line after the user presses
Enter.

■ *prompt* is the optional prompt INPUT displays on the
screen.

■ A semicolon after the prompt directs INPUT to display a
question mark after the prompt.

- A comma after the prompt directs INPUT to suppress the question mark.

- *variables* is the list of variables to input. Separate multiple variables with commas.

- If you enter a type other than the expected variable type or enter too many or too few values, INPUT displays the message *Redo from start*, and you must reenter the data.

- The user must separate multiple entries with commas.

Example:

```
'Question mark
INPUT "Enter your name and age"; uname$, age
PRINT uname$, age
'No question mark
INPUT "Enter your name and age", uname$, age
PRINT uname$, age
```

Related functions: INPUT$

Related statements: INPUT #; LINE INPUT

INPUT # Statement

Reads data from a sequential file.

Syntax:

INPUT #*file_number*, *variables*

Notes:

- *file_number* is the number assigned to the file in its OPEN statement.

- *variables* is the list of variables in which to store data from the file.

Example:

```
OPEN "SALARY.DAT" FOR INPUT AS #1
DO WHILE NOT EOF(1)
```

```
    INPUT #1, ename$, salary
    PRINT ename$, salary
LOOP
CLOSE #1
```

Related functions: INPUT$

Related statements: INPUT #; LINE INPUT

INPUT$ Function

Reads the specified number of characters from a file or the keyboard.

Syntax:

INPUT$(*num_characters* [, [#] *file_number*])

Notes:

■ *num_characters* is the number of characters for INPUT$ to read. It must be less than or equal to the record length of the file, which is 128 by default.

■ *file_number* is the number assigned to the file in its OPEN statement. If you omit a file number, INPUT$ reads from the keyboard.

Example:

```
'Display a file in UPPERCASE
OPEN "\CONFIG.SYS" FOR INPUT AS #1
DO WHILE NOT EOF(1)
    char$ = INPUT$(1, 1)
    PRINT UCASE$(char$);
LOOP
CLOSE #1
```

Related statements: INPUT; INPUT #; LINE INPUT

INSTR Function

Returns the location of the first occurrence of a string within another string.

Syntax:

INSTR([*startposition*], *searchstring*, *substring*)

Notes:

■ INSTR returns the character position of *substring* within *searchstring*.

■ *startposition* is the character position within *searchstring* where the search should begin. If you omit *startposition*, INSTR begins at position 1.

■ If INSTR locates the substring, it returns an index to the starting character. Otherwise, INSTR returns 0.

Example:

```
PRINT "RING in SUBSTRING", INSTR("SUBSTRING", "RING")
PRINT "X in STRING", INSTR("STRING", "X")
```

Running this program produces the following display:

```
RING in SUBSTRING 6
X in STRING       0
```

Related functions: LEFT$; LEN; MID$; RIGHT$

Related statements: MID$

INT Function

Returns the next integer value smaller than or equal to the specified numeric expression.

Syntax:

INT(*numeric_expression*)

Notes:

■ *numeric_expression* is any numeric expression.

Example:

```
PRINT INT(99.8), INT(99.1), INT(-99.2)
```

Running this program line produces the following display:

```
99       99      -100
```

Related functions: FIX

IOCTL Statement

Transmits a device control string to a device driver.

Syntax:

IOCTL [#]*file_number*, *control_string*

Notes:

■ *file_number* is the file number assigned to the device in its OPEN statement.

■ *control_string* is a string expression that specifies the command to send to the device.

■ For information on device control string information, refer to your hardware documentation.

Related functions: IOCTL$

IOCTL$ Function

Returns a control string from a device driver.

Syntax:

IOCTL$([#]*file_number*)

Notes:

■ *file_number* is the file number assigned to the device in its OPEN statement.

■ The information IOCTL$ returns is device dependent. For more information, see your hardware reference manual.

Related statements: IOCTL

KEY Statements

Assign string values to the function keys F1 through F12. Optionally, display the values of each key.

Syntax:

KEY *function_key*, *string_expression*

or

KEY LIST

or

KEY ON

or

KEY OFF

Notes:

■ *function_key* is the number of the desired function key. 1 corresponds to F1; 10 corresponds to F10. Use 30 and 31 to represent keys F11 and F12.

■ *string_expression* is a string of up to 15 characters that you want to assign to the function key.

■ Once you assign a string to a key, QBasic substitutes the string each time the user presses the corresponding function key.

- KEY LIST displays the entire 15-character assignment for each key.

- KEY ON displays across the bottom of the screen the first six letters of the strings assigned to keys F1 through F10.

- KEY OFF erases the display of the key assignments from the screen.

Example:

```
'Assign a string to F1
KEY 1, "F1 function key"
'Display key assignments
KEY ON
INPUT "Press the F1 key"; x$
PRINT x$
```

KEY(n) Statements

Enable or disable software trapping of specific keys.

Syntax:

KEY(n) **ON**

or

KEY(n) **OFF**

or

KEY(n) **STOP**

Notes:

- n is the number associated with a function key, a direction key, or a user-defined key:

Value of *n*	Meaning
1 through 10	Function keys F1 through F10
11	Up direction key
12	Left direction key
13	Right direction key
14	Down direction key
15 through 25	User-defined keys
30 and 31	Function keys F11 and F12

■ KEY(*n*) ON enables keyboard event trapping for the specified key.

■ KEY(*n*) OFF disables keyboard event trapping for the specified key. QBasic does not queue events that occur.

■ KEY(*n*) STOP inhibits event trapping for the specified key. Events are processed once trapping is enabled.

■ After you specify keyboard event trapping for a specific key, the ON *event* GOSUB statement enables keyboard trapping.

■ To declare a user-defined key, use the following variation of the KEY statement:

KEY *n*, **CHR$**(*keyboardflag*) + **CHR$**(*scancode*)

□ *n* is the number to associate with the user-defined key (15 through 25).

□ *keyboardflag* is one of the following values:

Flag	Meaning
0	No keyboard flag
1 through 3	Either Shift key*
4	Ctrl key
8	Alt key
32	Num Lock key
64	Caps Lock key
128	Extended keys on 101-key keyboard

*Key trapping does not distinguish between the left and right Shift keys.

☐ You can add the values together to test for multiple flags simultaneously.

☐ *scancode* is the scan code of the desired key.

Example:

```
ON KEY(10) GOSUB Handler
KEY(10) ON
PRINT "Press F10 to stop"
FOR i = 0 TO 100000
      PRINT i
NEXT i
Handler:
STOP
```

Related statements: ON *event* GOSUB

KILL Statement

Deletes a file from disk.

Syntax:

KILL *file_specification*

Notes:

■ *file_specification* is a string expression specifying the file to delete. The string can contain the MS-DOS wildcard characters ? and *.

Example:

```
KILL "TEST.DAT"
KILL "*.OLD"
```

Related statements: FILES

LBOUND Function

Returns the lowest array subscript for the specified array dimension.

Syntax:

LBOUND(*array_name*[, *dimension*])

Notes:

- *array_name* is the name of the array of interest.

- *dimension* is an integer value specifying the dimension of interest in a multidimensional array. The default is 1.

Example:

```
DIM a(50 TO 100) AS INTEGER
DIM box(1 TO 3, 3 TO 6) AS INTEGER

PRINT LBOUND(a)
PRINT LBOUND(box, 1), LBOUND(box, 2)
```

Running this program produces the following display:

```
50
1       3
```

Related functions: UBOUND

Related statements: DIM

LCASE$ Function

Returns a character string with all letters in the specified string expression in lowercase characters.

Syntax:

LCASE$(*string_expression*)

Notes:

■ *string_expression* is any string expression.

Example:

```
INPUT "Enter a string"; S$
PRINT LCASE$(S$)
```

Related functions: UCASE$

LEFT$ Function

Returns the specified number of characters beginning from the leftmost character of a string.

Syntax:

LEFT$(*string_expression*, *num_char*)

Notes:

■ *string_expression* is any string expression.

■ *num_char* is the number of characters to extract from the string. It must be in the range 0 through 32,767.

Example:

```
s$ = "TEST STRING"
FOR i = 1 TO LEN(s$)
    PRINT LEFT$(s$, i)
NEXT i
```

Related functions: INSTR; LEN; MID$; RIGHT$
Related statements: MID$

LEN Function

Returns the number of characters in a string or the number of bytes used to store a variable.

Syntax:

LEN(*string_expression*)

or

LEN(*variable*)

Notes:

■ *string_expression* is any string expression.

■ *variable* is any variable of a type other than STRING.

Example:

```
DIM x AS INTEGER, y AS LONG
a$ = "13 CHARACTERS"
PRINT a$, LEN(a$)
PRINT "Integer"; LEN(x), "Long"; LEN(y)
```

Running this program produces the following display:

```
13 CHARACTERS   13
Integer 2       Long 4
```

Related functions: INSTR; LEFT$; MID$; RIGHT$

Related statements: MID$

LET Statement

Assigns a value to a variable.

Syntax:

[**LET**] *variable* = *expression*

Notes:

■ LET is an optional keyword used in assignment statements to assign a value to a variable.

Example:

```
LET a = 5
'equivalent assignment without LET
a = 5
```

LINE Statement

Draws a line or box on the screen.

Syntax:

LINE [[**STEP**](*x1, y1*)]- [**STEP**](*x2, y2*)[,[*color*][, [B[F]]
[, *linestyle*]]]

Notes:

- LINE draws either a line using the coordinate pairs (*x1, y1*)
  and (*x2, y2*) as endpoints or a box with (*x1, y1*) as one
  corner and (*x2, y2*) as the opposite corner.

- The keyword STEP directs LINE to use the coordinates as
  an offset from the last point plotted as opposed to physical coordinates.

- *color* is the line or box color.

- B directs LINE to draw a box rather than a line.

- F directs LINE to fill the box with the specified color.

- *linestyle* is a 16-bit value whose bits determine whether or
  not pixels are drawn. By changing this value, you change
  the style of lines on your screen.

Example:

```
'Fill the screen with random boxes
SCREEN 1
FOR i = 1 TO 1000
     x1 = RND * 320
     y1 = RND * 200
     x2 = RND * 320
     y2 = RND * 200
     scolor = RND * 4
     LINE (x1, y1)-(x2, y2), scolor, BF
NEXT i
```

Related functions: POINT

Related statements: CIRCLE; COLOR; DRAW; PAINT;
PRESET; PSET; SCREEN

LINE INPUT Statement

Reads in a string of up to 255 characters.

Syntax:

LINE INPUT [;] ["*prompt*";] *string_variable*

or

LINE INPUT [#]*file_number*, *string_variable*

Notes:

■ Although the INPUT statement interprets a comma as a separator between two entries, the LINE INPUT statement does not. The LINE INPUT statement reads all characters up to the carriage return and assigns them to a string variable.

■ If present, the semicolon immediately following the keyword INPUT directs LINE INPUT to leave the cursor on the same line after the user presses Enter.

■ *prompt* is an optional message that directs the user to enter data.

■ *string_variable* is the string variable to which LINE INPUT assigns the information entered.

■ *file_number* is the file number assigned to the file in its OPEN statement.

Example:

```
LINE INPUT "Enter last name, first name, MI: "; fullname$
PRINT fullname$
```

Related functions: INPUT$

Related statements: INPUT; INPUT #

LOC Function

Returns the current offset or record number within a file.

Syntax:

LOC(*file_number*)

Notes:

- *file_number* is the file number assigned to the file in its OPEN statement.

- For binary files, LOC returns the current byte offset in the file. For random-access files, LOC returns the current record number. For sequential files, LOC returns the current offset, divided by 128. For a COM device, LOC returns the number of bytes in the input queue.

Example:

```
IF LOC(1) > 100 THEN CALL ReadIt(salary)
```

Related functions: SEEK
Related statements: SEEK

LOCATE Statement

Moves the cursor to the specified position on the screen and, optionally, sets the cursor size.

Syntax:

LOCATE [*row*][, [*column*][, [*visible*][, [*scan_start*][, *scan_stop*]]]]

Notes:

- *row* is the number of the desired row.
- *column* is the number of the desired column.

■ *visible,* when 1, causes the cursor to be displayed. When 0, it causes the cursor to be hidden.

■ *scan_start* is an integer specifying the first cursor scan line.

■ *scan_stop* is an integer specifying the last cursor scan line.

■ By changing the cursor scan lines, you can change the cursor size.

Example:

```
CLS
FOR i = 5 TO 20
    LOCATE i, i
    PRINT "Location is"; i; i
NEXT i
```

Related functions: CSRLIN; POS

LOCK Statement

Prevents access to all or specific portions of a file by network programs.

Syntax:

LOCK [#]*file_number* [,{*record* | [*start*] **TO** *end*}]

Notes:

■ *file_number* is the file number assigned to the file in its OPEN statement.

■ For random-access files, LOCK locks the specified record or range of records. For binary files, LOCK locks the specified byte or range of bytes. For sequential files, LOCK locks the entire file.

■ LOCK is necessary only in network environments.

■ If a network program tries to access a locked record or byte, QBasic generates an error.

- To use LOCK, you should first run the SHARE.EXE program, an MS-DOS program that supports file sharing and locking.

Example:

```
INPUT "Enter record number to update"; rec
LOCK #1, rec         'Restrict access
emp.name$ = "SMITH"
PUT #1, rec
UNLOCK rec           'Allow access
```

Related statements: UNLOCK

LOF Function

Returns the number of bytes in a file.

Syntax:

LOF(*file_number*)

Notes:

- *file_number* is the file number assigned to the file in its OPEN statement.

- You cannot use LOF with devices.

Example:

```
OPEN "\CONFIG.SYS" FOR INPUT AS #1
PRINT "File size in bytes is"; LOF(1)
CLOSE #1
```

LOG Function

Returns the natural logarithm of a numeric expression.

Syntax:

LOG(*numeric_expression*)

Notes:

■ *numeric_expression* is any numeric expression greater than 0.

■ The natural logarithm is the logarithm to the base *e*.

Example:

```
PRINT LOG(1), LOG(EXP(1))
```

Running this program produces the following display:

```
0               1
```

Related functions: EXP

LPOS Function

Returns the current position of the printer head within a print buffer.

Syntax:

LPOS(*printer_number*)

Notes:

■ *printer_number* is the number of the printer of interest. 1 is LPT1, 2 is LPT2, and so on.

■ Not all printers support LPOS.

Example:

```
FOR i = 1 TO 100
    LPRINT i;                          'Print number on same line
    IF LPOS(1) > 50 THEN LPRINT        'Start a new line
NEXT i
```

LPRINT Statement

Prints on the printer LPT1.

Syntax:

LPRINT [*output_list*][{; | ,}]

Notes:

■ *output_list* is a list of numeric and string expressions to be printed. Expressions must be separated by commas or semicolons.

■ A semicolon following the output list leaves the print head at the next character position. A comma leaves the print head at the next print zone. Print zones are 14 characters in length. Omitting a semicolon or comma causes the printer to advance to the beginning of the next line.

Example:

```
LPRINT "This is on line 1"
LPRINT "This is on";
LPRINT " line 2"
```

Running this program produces the following display:

```
This is on line 1
This is on line 2
```

Related statements: LPRINT USING; WIDTH

LPRINT USING Statement

Prints formatted output on the printer LPT1.

Syntax:

LPRINT USING *format_string*; *output_list*[{; | ,}]

Notes:

- *format_string* is the output format. See PRINT USING for a list of formatting characters.

- *output_list* is a list of numeric and string expressions to be printed. Expressions must be separated by commas or semicolons.

- A semicolon following the output list leaves the print head at the next character position. A comma leaves the print head at the next print zone. Print zones are 14 characters in length. Omitting a semicolon or comma causes the printer to advance to the beginning of the next line.

Example:

See PRINT USING

Related statements: LPRINT; PRINT USING; WIDTH

LSET Statement

Moves data into a random-access file buffer, assigns a variable of one record type to a variable of a different record type, or left-justifies the value of a string variable.

Syntax:

LSET *string_variable* = *string_expression*

or

LSET *record_variable1* = *record_variable2*

Notes:

■ *string_variable* is either a random-access file field or a string variable.

■ *string_expression* is any string expression.

■ *record_variable1* and *record_variable2* are user-defined record variables.

Example:

```
salary = 66000
LSET e$ = MKS$(salary)
PUT #1
```

Related statements: RSET

LTRIM$ Function

Removes the leading blank characters from a string expression.

Syntax:

LTRIM$(*string_expression*)

Notes:

■ *string_expression* is any string expression.

Example:

```
PRINT LTRIM$("    Trim test")
```

Running this program line produces the following display:

```
Trim test
```

Related functions: RTRIM$

MID$ Function

Returns a substring of a string expression that begins at the specified offset location.

Syntax:

MID$(*string_expression*, *start_offset* [, *length*])

Notes:

- *string_expression* is any string expression.
- *start_offset* is the position of the first character of the substring.
- *length* is the number of characters in the substring. If you omit *length*, MID$ returns all characters from *start_offset* through the end of the string.

Example:

```
a$ = "ABCDEFGHI"
PRINT MID$(a$, 1, 5)
PRINT MID$(a$, 6)
```

Running this program produces the following display:

```
ABCDE
FGHI
```

Related functions: INSTR; LEFT$; LEN; RIGHT$

Related statements: MID$

MID$ Statement

Replaces a portion of a string with another string.

Syntax:

MID$(*string_variable*, *start_offset*[, *num_char*]) = *string_expression*

Notes:

- *string_variable* is the string variable to be modified.

- *start_offset* is the position of the first character to be replaced in the string variable.

- *num_char* is the number of characters in the string to replace. If you omit this value, MID$ uses the length of the replacement string.

- *string_expression* is any string expression.

Example:

```
a$ = "ABCDEF"
MID$(a$, 2, 2) = "bc"
PRINT a$
```

Running this program produces the following display:

```
AbcDEF
```

Related functions: INSTR; LEFT$; LEN; MID$; RIGHT$

MKD$ Function

Converts a double-precision value to an 8-byte string for output to a random-access file by PUT.

Syntax:

MKD$(*numeric_expression*)

Notes:

- *numeric_expression* is a double-precision numeric expression.

Example:

```
OPEN "TEST.DAT" FOR RANDOM AS #1 LEN=8
FIELD #1, 8 AS sal$
salary = 60000
```

```
sal$ = MKD$(salary)
PUT #1
CLOSE #1
```

Related functions: CVD; CVI; CVL; CVS; CVDMBF; CVSMBF; MKDMBF$; MKI$; MKL$; MKS$; MKSMBF$

MKDIR Statement

Creates the specified MS-DOS subdirectory.

Syntax:

MKDIR *directory_name*

Notes:

■ *directory_name* is a string expression that specifies the subdirectory to create.

Example:

```
ON ERROR GOTO CheckExists
MKDIR "TESTDIR"
PRINT "Directory TESTDIR created"
Done:
END
CheckExists:
    IF ERR = 75 THEN
        PRINT "Directory TESTDIR already exists"
        RESUME Done
    END IF
    ON ERROR GOTO 0
```

Related statements: CHDIR; RMDIR

MKDMBF$ Function

Converts a double-precision value stored in IEEE format to an 8-byte string containing the value in Microsoft binary format for output to a random-access file by PUT.

Syntax:

MKDMBF$(*numeric_expression*)

Notes:

■ *numeric_expression* is a double-precision numeric expression.

■ CVDMBF, CVSMBF, MKDMBF$, and MKSMBF$ are useful for maintaining data files created with earlier versions of Basic.

Example:

See MKSMBF$

Related functions: CVD, CVDMBF; CVI; CVL; CVS; CVSMBF; MKD$; MKI$; MKL$; MKS$; MKSMBF$

MKI$ Function

Converts an integer value to a 2-byte string for output to a random-access file by PUT.

Syntax:

MKI$(*numeric_expression*)

Notes:

■ *numeric_expression* is an integer numeric expression.

Example:

See MKD$

Related functions: CVD; CVDMBF$; CVI; CVL; CVS; CVSMBF$; MKD$; MKDMBF$; MKL$; MKS$; MKSMBF$

MKL$ Function

Converts a long integer value to a 4-byte string for output to a random-access file by PUT.

Syntax:

MKL$(*numeric_expression*)

Notes:

■ *numeric_expression* is a long integer numeric expression.

Example:

See MKD$

Related functions: CVD; CVDMBF; CVI; CVL; CVS; CVSMBF; MKD$; MKDMBF$; MKI$; MKS$; MKSMBF$

MKS$ Function

Converts a single-precision value to a 4-byte string for output to a random-access file by PUT.

Syntax:

MKS$(*numeric_expression*)

Notes:

■ *numeric_expression* is a single-precision numeric expression.

Example:

See MKD$

Related functions: CVD; CVDMBF; CVI; CVL; CVS; CVSMBF; MKD$; MKDMBF$; MKI$; MKL$; MKSMBF$

MKSMBF$ Function

Converts a single-precision value stored in IEEE format to a
4-byte string containing the value in Microsoft binary format
for output to a random-access file by PUT.

Syntax:

MKSMBF$(*numeric_expression*)

Notes:

■ *numeric_expression* is a single-precision numeric
expression.

■ CVDMBF, CVSMBF, MKDMBF$, and MKSMBF$ are
useful for maintaining data files created with earlier
versions of Basic.

Example:

```
TYPE EmpRec
    ename AS STRING * 20
    salary AS STRING * 4
END TYPE

DIM employee AS EmpRec
OPEN "SALARY.DAT" FOR RANDOM AS #1 LEN=LEN(employee)
employee.ename = "Jones"
employee.salary = MKSMBF$(65000)
PUT #1, 1, employee
CLOSE #1
```

Related functions: CVDMBF; CVSMBF; MKDMBF$

NAME Statement

Renames a file or directory on disk.

Syntax:

NAME *oldfile_name* **AS** *newfile_name*

Notes:

- *oldfile_name* is a string expression containing the name of an existing MS-DOS file.

- *newfile_name* is a string expression containing the desired filename. A file with this name cannot already exist on disk.

- *newfile_name* must be on the same disk as *oldfile_name*.

Example:

```
NAME "OLDFILE.DAT" AS "NEWFILE.DAT"
```

Related statements: FILES

OCT$ Function

Returns a string containing the octal representation of an integer expression.

Syntax:

OCT$(*numeric_expression*)

Notes:

- Octal is the base-8 numbering system.

- *numeric_expression* is any numeric expression.

Example:

See HEX$

Related functions: HEX$

ON ERROR GOTO Statement

Enables error handling and specifies the first line of the error handler.

Syntax:

ON ERROR GOTO *location*

Notes:

- See ERR for a list of possible errors.

- *location* is the line number or label of the first line in the handler. A line number of 0 disables error handling.

- If error handling is disabled, an error results in an error message and program termination.

Example:

```
ON ERROR GOTO Handler
OPEN "NOFILE.DAT" FOR INPUT AS #1
PRINT "File opened"
CLOSE #1
Done:
END
Handler:
     IF ERR = 53 THEN
          PRINT "File not found"
     END IF
     RESUME Done
```

Related functions: ERDEV; ERDEV$; ERL; ERR

Related statements: ERROR; RESUME

ON *event* GOSUB Statements

Specify the first line of an event-trapping subroutine.

Syntax:

ON COM(*n*) **GOSUB** *location*

or

ON KEY(*n*) **GOSUB** *location*

or

ON PEN GOSUB *location*

or

ON PLAY(*queuesize*) **GOSUB** *location*

or

ON STRIG(*n*) **GOSUB** *location*

or

ON TIMER(*n*) **GOSUB** *location*

Notes:

- The ON COM(*n*) GOSUB statement branches to the subroutine whenever characters are received at the specified serial port.

- The ON KEY(*n*) GOSUB statement branches to the subroutine whenever the key associated with the specified number is pressed.

- The ON PEN GOSUB statement branches to the subroutine whenever the light pen is activated.

- The ON PLAY(*queuesize*) GOSUB statement branches to the subroutine whenever the number of notes in the music buffer goes from *queuesize* to *queuesize* − 1. The variable *queuesize* must be in the range 1 through 32.

- The ON STRIG(*n*) GOSUB statement branches to the subroutine whenever the specified joystick button is pressed. See STRIG statement for valid values for *n*.

- The ON TIMER(*n*) GOSUB statement branches to the subroutine whenever the specified number of seconds have passed. The number of seconds must be in the range 1 through 86,400.

- These statements do not enable event trapping; they only associate a subroutine with an event.

Example:

```
ON KEY(10) GOSUB DisplayHelp
KEY(10) ON

PRINT "Press F10 for help"
DO
      INPUT "Enter name"; n$
      PRINT n$
LOOP UNTIL n$ = "QUIT"
END

DisplayHelp:
      PRINT "Type QUIT at name prompt"
      RETURN
```

Related statements: COM; KEY(*n*); PEN; PLAY (Event Trapping); STRIG; TIMER

ON *expression* **Statements**

Branch to one of several locations based on the result of an expression.

Syntax:

ON *numeric_expression* **GOSUB** *location*[, *location*]...

or

ON *numeric_expression* **GOTO** *location*[, *location*]...

Notes:

■ *numeric_expression* is any numeric expression in the range 0 through 255. If necessary, QBasic rounds the expression to an integer value.

■ *location* is the list of line numbers or labels to which control should branch. If the result of the numeric expression is 1, control branches to the first location. If the expression is 2, control branches to the second location, and so on. If the value does not have a corresponding label, execution continues at the next statement.

Example:

```
FOR i = 1 TO 3
    ON i GOSUB One, Two, Three
NEXT i
END
One:
    PRINT "In One"
    RETURN
Two:
    PRINT "In Two"
    RETURN
Three:
    PRINT "In Three"
    RETURN
```

Related statements: DO UNTIL; DO WHILE; GOSUB; GOTO

OPEN Statement

Opens a file or device for input or output operations.

Syntax:

OPEN *filename* [**FOR** *access_mode*] [**ACCESS** *network_access*]
    [*lock_type*] **AS** [#]*file_number* [**LEN**=*record_length*]

or

OPEN *mode*, [#]*file_number*, *filename*[, *record_length*]

or

OPEN "**COM***n*: *basic_com com_specifics*" [**FOR** *access_mode*]
    AS [#]*file_number* [**LEN**=*record_length*]

Notes:

■ *filename* is a string expression containing the name of the file or device to open.

■ *access_mode* specifies how the file is to be used: INPUT, OUTPUT, APPEND, RANDOM, or BINARY. The default is RANDOM.

- *network_access* provides more detail on how the file is to be used in shared-file network environments: READ, WRITE, or READ WRITE.

- *lock_type* is the type of file locking used in shared-file environments: SHARED, LOCK READ, LOCK WRITE, or LOCK READ WRITE.

- *file_number* is the integer number to associate with the file for read, write, and close operations.

- *record_length* is the number of bytes in each record. For sequential files, the default is 512; for random-access files, the default is 128; for communications, the default is 128. The value cannot exceed 32,767.

- *mode* is used for older Basic programs. It is a single-letter string that specifies the access mode:

Option	Mode
A	Append
B	Binary
I	Input
O	Output
R	Random

- *n* is the number of the communications port to open, either 1 or 2.

- *basic_com* represents the basic data-communications parameters, separated by commas, in the following form:

  [*baud*][, [*parity*][, [*databits*][, [*stopbits*]]]]

  □ *baud* is the baud rate of the device used: 75, 110, 150, 300, 600, 1200, 1800, 2400, 4800, 9600, or 19200.

  □ *parity* is the parity of the device used: N (none), E (even), O (odd), S (space), M (mark), or PE (enable error checking).

    ☐ *databits* is the number of bits in each data word: 5, 6, 7, or 8. The sum of parity bits and data bits must be less than or equal to 8. If the parity is set to O (odd) or E (even), one bit is used for parity. If parity is set to N (none), no bits are used for parity.

    ☐ *stopbits* is the number of stop bits for each word: 1, 1.5, or 2.

■ *com_specifics* is a list of data-communications specifics, separated by commas:

Option	Purpose
ASC	Opens device in ASCII mode
BIN	Opens device in binary mode
CD[*milliseconds*]	Specifies carrier-detect timeout
CS[*milliseconds*]	Specifies clear-to-send timeout
DS[*milliseconds*]	Specifies data-set-ready timeout
LF	Sends linefeed after each carriage return
OP[*milliseconds*]	Specifies the OPEN statement timeout period
RB[*bytes*]	Specifies the size of the receive buffer
RS	Suppresses detection of Request To Send (RTS)
TB[*bytes*]	Specifies the size of the transmit buffer

Example:

```
OPEN "TEST.DAT" FOR INPUT AS #1

f% = FREEFILE
OPEN "NEW.DAT" FOR RANDOM AS f% LEN = 80

OPEN "COM1:4800, E, 7, 1, BIN" AS #2
```

Related functions: FREEFILE

Related statements: CLOSE

OPTION BASE Statement

Sets the default lower array bound.

Syntax:

OPTION BASE {0 |1}

Notes:

- If you don't specify a default lower bound, QBasic uses 0.
- You can specify only one OPTION BASE statement per module.
- For more flexibility, use the TO clause in the DIM statement.

Example:

```
OPTION BASE 0
DIM a(1 TO 20)
DIM b(20)
PRINT LBOUND(a), LBOUND(b)
PRINT UBOUND(a), UBOUND(b)
```

Running this program produces the following display:

```
1        0
20       20
```

Related functions: LBOUND; UBOUND

Related statements: DIM; REDIM

OUT Statement

Sends a byte to the specified port.

Syntax:

OUT *port_number, byte_value*

Notes:

- *port_number* is an integer expression in the range 0 through 65,535 that identifies the port.

- *byte_value* is an integer expression in the range 0 through 255 to send to the port.

Example:

See INP

Related functions: INP

PAINT Statement

Fills a graphics screen image with the specified color or pattern.

Syntax:

PAINT [STEP](*x*, *y*)[, [{*color* | *tile*}][, [*bordercolor*][, *background*]]]

Notes:

- The keyword STEP indicates that *x* and *y* are offsets from the current graphics position as opposed to physical coordinates.

- *x*, *y* is a set of coordinates within the graphics image.

- *color* is the desired fill color. If you omit *color*, PAINT uses the current foreground color.

- *tile* is a fill pattern 8 bits wide and up to 64 bits long that is defined as follows:

  *tile$* = CHR$(*n*) [+CHR$(*n*)]...

  where the values of *n* are integers between 0 and 255. Each CHR$(*n*) defines a 1-byte, 8-pixel slice of the fill pattern based on the binary form of the number.

- *bordercolor* is the color of the border surrounding the graphics image. If you omit *bordercolor*, PAINT uses *color*.

- *background* is a one-character string that specifies a background pattern that can be painted over. If you omit *background*, PAINT uses CHR$(0).

Example:

```
SCREEN 1
LINE (10, 10)-(50, 50), 1, B
PAINT (11, 11), 2, 1
```

Related functions: POINT

Related statements: CIRCLE; COLOR; DRAW; LINE; PRESET; PSET; SCREEN

PALETTE, PALETTE USING
Statements

Change one or more colors in the color palette.

Syntax:

PALETTE [*change_color, new_color*]

or

PALETTE USING *array*[(*index*)]

Notes:

- *change_color* is the attribute to change.
- *new_color* is the new color to assign to the attribute.
- *array* is an array of color numbers to assign to the attributes available in the current screen mode.

- *index* is the index of the first element in the array to use in setting the palette.

- If you omit all arguments, PALETTE restores the default color values.

Example:

```
PALETTE 0, 1
```

Related statements: COLOR; SCREEN

PCOPY Statement

Copies one video display page to another.

Syntax:

PCOPY *source_page*, *target_page*

Notes:

- *source_page* is an integer expression that specifies the video display page to be copied.

- *target_page* is an integer expression that specifies the video display page to which the source page is to be copied.

- The number of video display pages available is dependent on the video memory size and video display mode.

Example:

```
'Copy video page 1 to page 3
PCOPY 1, 3
```

PEEK Function

Returns the byte stored at a specific memory offset.

Syntax:

PEEK(*offset*)

Notes:

■ *offset* is an integer expression (in the range 0 through 65,535) that specifies an offset within the current default segment.

■ The DEF SEG statement defines the default segment address.

Example:

```
'Save the screen's contents
DIM screensave(3999) AS INTEGER
DEF SEG = &HB800
FOR i = 0 TO 3999
    screensave(i) = PEEK(i)
NEXT i
DEF SEG
```

Related statements: DEF SEG; POKE

PEN Function

Returns the light pen coordinates.

Syntax:

PEN(*numeric_expression*)

Notes:

■ *numeric_expression* is an integer value (in the range 0 through 9) that specifies the information PEN returns:

Value	Returns
0	−1 if pen used since last call; otherwise 0
1	The x pixel coordinate where pen was last pressed
2	The y pixel coordinate where pen was last pressed
3	Current usage: −1 if down; 0 if up
4	The last known x pixel value
5	The last known y pixel value
6	Character row where pen was last pressed
7	Character column where pen was last pressed
8	The last known character row
9	The last known character column

■ PEN does not work when a mouse driver is active.

Example:

```
row% = PEN(6)
column% = PEN(7)
```

PEN Statements

Enable or disable light pen event trapping.

Syntax:

PEN ON

or

PEN OFF

or

PEN STOP

Notes:

■ The PEN ON statement enables light pen event trapping.

■ The PEN OFF statement disables light pen event trapping. All light pen events are ignored.

- The PEN STOP statement temporarily suspends light pen
  event trapping. All light pen events occurring during this
  period are processed after event trapping is enabled.

Example:

```
ON PEN GOSUB Handler
PEN ON
```

Related functions: PEN

Related statements: ON *event* GOSUB

PLAY Function

Returns the number of notes in the background music queue.

Syntax:

PLAY(*dummy_argument*)

Notes:

- *dummy_argument* is any numeric argument. It simply dis-
  tinguishes the PLAY function from the PLAY statement.

- PLAY returns 0 when music is in foreground mode.

Example:

```
notes% = PLAY(0)
```

Related statements: ON *event* GOSUB; PLAY;
PLAY (Event Trapping); SOUND

PLAY Statement

Plays the tune specified by a string expression.

Syntax:

PLAY *string_expression*

Notes:

■ *string_expression* is a string expression that contains one or more of the following commands:

Octave commands

>	Increases octave by 1 to a maximum of 6.
<	Decreases octave by 1 to a minimum of 0.
O *level*	Sets the current octave; *level* must be 0 through 6. Default is 4.

Duration commands

L *notetype*	Sets the length of each note from 1 to 64; 1 is whole, 2 is half, and so on. Default is 4.
ML	Sets music legato.
MN	Sets music normal. This is the default.
MS	Sets music staccato.

Mode commands

MF	Sets music to foreground. This is the default.
MB	Sets music to background. Up to 32 notes can play as the program executes.

Temp commands

P *duration*	Specifies a pause from 1 to 64; 1 is whole, 2 is half, and so on.
T *notes*	Sets the tempo from 32 to 255. Default is 120.

Tone commands

A–G	Plays the note specified.
N *note*	Plays a note from 0 to 84; 0 is a rest.

Suffix commands

# or +	Turns a note into a sharp.
–	Turns a note into a flat.
.	Plays the note 3/2 as long as specified.

■ The string expression "X"+VARPTR$(*string*) executes the music substring *string*.

Example:

```
'Play scale in 7 different octaves
scale$ = "CDEFGAB"
PLAY "L16"
FOR i = 0 TO 6
     PLAY "O" + STR$(i)
     PLAY "X" + VARPTR$(scale$)
NEXT i
```

Related functions: PLAY

Related statements: ON *event* GOSUB; PLAY
(Event Trapping); SOUND

PLAY Statements (Event Trapping)

Enable or disable play event trapping.

Syntax:

PLAY ON

or

PLAY OFF

or

PLAY STOP

Notes:

■ PLAY ON enables play event trapping.

■ PLAY OFF disables play event trapping. All events that occur are ignored.

■ PLAY STOP temporarily suspends play event trapping. All play events are processed after play event trapping is enabled.

Example:

```
ON PLAY GOSUB Handler
PLAY ON
```

Related functions: PLAY

Related statements: ON *event* GOSUB; PLAY

PMAP Function

Maps a physical coordinate to a logical coordinate defined by the WINDOW statement or vice versa.

Syntax:

PMAP(*coordinate*, *mapping*)

Notes:

■ *coordinate* is a numeric expression of the coordinate to be mapped.

■ *mapping* specifies the type of conversion:

Value	Maps
0	Logical coordinate to physical x
1	Logical coordinate to physical y
2	Physical coordinate to logical x
3	Physical coordinate to logical y

Example:

```
SCREEN 1
WINDOW SCREEN (0, 0)-(100, 100)
'Convert logical to physical
x = PMAP(50, 0)
y = PMAP(50, 1)
```

Related statements: VIEW; WINDOW

POINT Function

Returns a pixel's color or coordinates.

Syntax:

POINT(*x*, *y*)

or

POINT(*mapping*)

Notes:

■ The POINT(*x*, *y*) function returns the color of the pixel at the *x*, *y* coordinate.

■ The POINT(*mapping*) function returns the coordinates of the graphics cursor based on the value of *mapping*.

Value	Returns
0	Physical *x* coordinate
1	Physical *y* coordinate
2	Logical *x* coordinate
3	Logical *y* coordinate

Example:

```
x% = POINT(0)
y% = POINT(1)
pcolor% = POINT(x%, y%)
```

Related statements: CIRCLE; COLOR; DRAW; LINE; PAINT; PRESET; PSET; SCREEN

POKE Statement

Places a byte in the specified memory location.

Syntax:

POKE *offset*, *byte_value*

Notes:

- *offset* is the offset (from 0 through 65,535) within the current segment where you want to place the byte.

- *byte_value* is the value (from 0 through 255) to poke into memory.

Example:

```
'Fill CGA screen with A's
DEF SEG = &HB800
FOR i = 0 TO 3999
    IF i MOD 2 = 0 THEN
        POKE i, 65      'letter A
    ELSE
        POKE i, 7       'display attribute
    END IF
NEXT i
DEF SEG
```

Related functions: PEEK

Related statements: DEF SEG

POS Function

Returns the cursor column position.

Syntax:

POS(*dummy_argument*)

Notes:

- POS does not use the parameter *dummy_argument*.

Example:

```
FOR i = 1 TO 100
    IF (POS(0) > 50) THEN
        PRINT i
    ELSE
        PRINT i; 'same line
    END IF
NEXT i
```

Related functions: CSRLIN; LPOS
Related statements: LOCATE

PRESET Statement

Draws a pixel at the specified screen coordinates.

Syntax:

PRESET [**STEP**](x, y)[, *color*]

Notes:

- The keyword STEP indicates that x and y are offsets from the last point drawn, as opposed to actual coordinates.

- PRESET is similar to PSET, except that if you omit *color*, PRESET uses the background color.

- If the coordinates are outside the current viewport, no point is drawn.

Example:

See PSET

Related functions: POINT

Related statements: CIRCLE; COLOR; DRAW; LINE; PAINT; PSET

PRINT Statement

Writes to the screen or a sequential file.

Syntax:

PRINT [#*file_number*,] [*output_list*][{; | ,}]

Notes:

■ *file_number* is the number of the file to which output is written. If you omit *file_number*, QBasic writes the data to the screen.

■ *output_list* is a list of one or more expressions to output. The expressions can be string or numeric.

■ If a semicolon ends the PRINT line, the next PRINT statement continues on the same line in the next character position. If a comma ends the line, the next PRINT statement continues on the same line in the next print zone. Print zones are 14 characters in length. Omitting a semicolon or comma causes the next PRINT statement to begin on the next line.

Example:

```
PRINT "This is line"; 1
PRINT "This is line";
PRINT 2
PRINT "This is line", 3
PRINT "This is line",
PRINT 4
```

Running this program produces the following display:

```
This is line 1
This is line 2
This is line   3
This is line   4
```

Related statements: LPRINT; LPRINT USING; PRINT USING

PRINT USING Statement

Writes formatted output to the screen display or a file.

Syntax:

PRINT [#]*file_number,*] **USING** *format_list*; *output_list*[{; | ,}]

Notes:

- *file_number* is the number of the file to which output is written. If you omit *file_number*, QBasic writes the data to the screen.

- *format_list* is a string expression containing one or more of the following format specifiers:

Specifier	Result
!	Displays only the first character in a string
\ \	Prints 2 + *n* characters of a string, where *n* is the number of spaces between the backslashes
&	Displays a string of any length
#	Represents a digit position
.	Represents the decimal point position
+	Displays a plus sign for positive values and a minus sign for negative values
−	Appends a trailing minus sign to a negative number if symbol appears at the end of a numeric field
**	Replaces leading blanks with asterisks in a numeric field
$$	Precedes a numeric value with a dollar sign
**$	Replaces leading blanks with asterisks in a numeric field and precedes the value with a dollar sign
,	Places a comma after every third digit if symbol appears to the left of the decimal point
^^^^	Displays a value in exponential format
_ *n*	Prints the character *n* as a literal character as opposed to a format character
n	Prints the character *n* if not listed above

Example:

```
a = 123.4567
PRINT USING "###.##"; a
PRINT USING "+###.####"; a
```

```
a$ = "ABCDEFG"
PRINT USING "!"; a$
PRINT USING "\ \"; a$
```

Running this program produces the following result:

```
123.45
+123.4567
A
ABCD
```

Related statements: LPRINT; LPRINT USING; PRINT

PSET Statement

Draws a pixel at the specified screen coordinates.

Syntax:

PSET [**STEP**](*x*, *y*) [, *color*]

Notes:

■ The keyword STEP indicates that *x* and *y* are offsets from the last point drawn, as opposed to coordinates.

■ *color* is the desired pixel color. If you omit *color*, PSET uses the current foreground color.

■ If the coordinates are outside the current viewport, no point is drawn.

Example:

```
SCREEN 1
COLOR 1, 2
CLS
FOR i = 1 TO 10000
    PSET(RND * 320, RND * 200), RND * 4
NEXT i
```

Related functions: POINT

Related statements: CIRCLE; COLOR; DRAW; LINE; PAINT; PRESET; SCREEN

PUT Statement (File I/O)

Writes a random-access file buffer or record variable to a file.

Syntax:

PUT [#] *file_number*[, [*record_number*][, *variable*]]

Notes:

- *file_number* is the file number assigned to the file in its OPEN statement.

- *record_number* is the record number (from 1 through 2,147,483,647) in a random-access file or the byte offset in a binary file.

- *variable* is a variable containing the fields of the record.

Example:

```
TYPE Employee
    ename AS STRING * 20
    salary AS SINGLE
END TYPE

DIM emp AS Employee
OPEN "SALARY.DAT" FOR RANDOM AS #1 LEN=LEN(emp)
emp.ename = "Parrish"
emp.salary = 50000
PUT #1, 1, emp
CLOSE #1
```

Related functions: CVD; CVDMBF; CVI; CVL; CVS; CVSMBF; MKD$; MKDMBF$; MKI$; MKL$; MKS$; MKSMBF$

Related statements: GET; LSET; OPEN; RSET

PUT Statement (Graphics)

Displays a graphics image on the screen.

Syntax:

PUT [**STEP**](*x*, *y*),*array*[(*index*)][, *display_verb*]

Notes:

■ The keyword STEP indicates that *x* and *y* are offsets from the last point drawn, as opposed to physical coordinates.

■ *array* is the name of the array containing the image to display.

■ *index* is the index where the graphics image begins in the array.

■ *display_verb* indicates how the image is displayed:

Verb	Action
PSET	Colors remain unchanged
PRESET	Colors are inverted
AND	A logical AND with an existing image in the same location
OR	A logical OR with an existing image in the same location
XOR	An exclusive OR of an existing image on the screen (useful for animation)

Example:

```
SCREEN 1
DIM box(1 TO 200)
x1 = 0
x2 = 10
y1 = 0
y2 = 10
LINE (x1, y1)-(x2, y2), 2, BF        'Create a box
GET (x1, y1)-(x2, y2), box           'Save image
```

```
FOR i = 1 TO 10000
     PUT (x1, y1), box, XOR          'Move box around
     x1 = RND * 300                  'screen randomly
     y1 = RND * 180
     PUT (x1, y1), box
NEXT i
```

Related statements: GET (Graphics); SCREEN

RANDOMIZE Statement

Initializes the random number generator.

Syntax:

RANDOMIZE [*seed*]

Notes:

■ *seed* is an integer expression that initializes the random
   number generator. If you omit *seed*, RANDOMIZE
   prompts the user to enter it.

Example:

```
'Print fifty random numbers
'using ten different seeds
FOR i = 1 TO 10
     PRINT "Seed"; i
     RANDOMIZE i
     FOR j = 1 TO 5
          PRINT RND
     NEXT j
NEXT i
```

Related functions: RND; TIMER

READ Statement

Reads values from a data list and assigns them to variables.

Syntax:

READ *variable_list*

Notes:

■ *variable_list* is a list of variables separated by commas. READ and DATA statements work hand in hand to assign values to these variables.

Example:

```
READ n$, age, salary
READ address$
DATA "Kellie", 21, 500
DATA "Las Vegas, Nevada"
PRINT n$, age, salary
PRINT address$
```

Related statements: DATA; RESTORE

REDIM Statement

Changes the size of a dynamic array.

Syntax:

REDIM [**SHARED**] *array(subscripts)* [**AS** *typename*]
    [, *array(subscripts)* [**AS** *typename*]]...

Notes:

■ You can change the size of a dynamic array but not the number of dimensions or the data type.

■ The keyword SHARED indicates that the array can be used by all procedures in the module.

■ *array* is the name of the array to resize.

- *subscripts* specifies the array subscripts in the form

  [*lowerbound* **TO**] *upperbound*

- Multidimensional arrays are supported.

- *typename* is the array type: INTEGER, LONG, SINGLE, DOUBLE, STRING, or a user-defined type.

- REDIM erases the array's previous values.

Example:

```
'$DYNAMIC
DIM box (1 TO 100)
'statements
REDIM box (1 TO 200)
```

Related statements: DIM; ERASE

REM Statement

Allows explanatory comments or remarks on a program line.

Syntax:

REM *comment*

Notes:

- *comment* is any text.

- QBasic ignores comment lines unless they contain compiler metacommands.

- QBasic supports the use of a single quotation mark (') instead of the REM statement.

Example:

```
REM This is a comment
'This is a comment
```

RESET Statement

Writes on disk any data still in the file buffers and closes all disk files.

Syntax:

RESET

Notes:

■ RESET closes all open files at once. You can use the CLOSE statement to close files individually.

Example:

RESET

Related statements: CLOSE; OPEN

RESTORE Statement

Allows READ to reuse a previously read DATA statement.

Syntax:

RESTORE [*location*]

Notes:

■ *location* is the line number or label of the DATA statement to read next. If you omit *location*, the next READ uses the first DATA statement in the program.

Example:

```
FOR i = 1 TO 5
    READ a%, b%, c%
    PRINT a%, b%, c%
```

```
     RESTORE
NEXT i
DATA 1, 2, 3
```

Related statements: DATA; READ

RESUME Statement

Continues program execution from an error-trapping handler.

Syntax:

RESUME [*location*]

or

RESUME NEXT

Notes:

■ *location* is the line number or label at which execution should continue. If you specify 0 or omit *location*, execution continues at the statement causing the error.

■ The keyword NEXT continues execution at the statement immediately following the statement causing the error.

Example:

```
ON ERROR GOTO Handler
OPEN "A:TEST.DAT" FOR INPUT AS #1
'statements
END

Handler:
     PRINT "Place disk containing TEST.DAT"
     PRINT "in drive A.  Press Enter."
     INPUT dummy$
     RESUME
```

Related statements: ERROR; ON ERROR GOTO

RETURN Statement

Returns control from a subroutine to the calling procedure.

Syntax:

RETURN [*location*]

Notes:

- *location* is the line number or label at which execution should continue. If you omit *location*, execution continues at the line following the GOSUB statement or, for event handling, at the line at which an event occurred.

Example:

```
GOSUB One
GOSUB Two
END

One:
     PRINT "In One"
     RETURN

Two:
     PRINT "In Two"
     RETURN
```

Related statements: GOSUB; ON *event* GOSUB

RIGHT$ Function

Returns the specified number of characters from the rightmost characters in a string.

Syntax:

RIGHT$(*string_expression, num_char*)

Notes:

■ *string_expression* is any string expression.

■ *num_char* is the number of characters to return. If *num_char* exceeds the length of the string, RIGHT$ returns the entire string.

Example:

```
A$ = "ABCDEFGHIJ"
FOR I = 1 TO 10
    PRINT RIGHT$(A$, I)
NEXT I
```

Related functions: INSTR; LEFT$; LEN; MID$

RMDIR Statement

Removes the specified subdirectory.

Syntax:

RMDIR *directory_name*

Notes:

■ *directory_name* is a string expression containing the name of the directory to delete.

■ RMDIR works like the MS-DOS RMDIR command. It cannot delete the current directory or a directory containing files.

Example:

```
RMDIR "A:\TEST"
```

Related statements: CHDIR; MKDIR

RND Function

Returns a single-precision random number between 0 and 1.

Syntax:

RND[(*numeric_expression*)]

Notes:

- *numeric_expression* specifies how RND generates the next random number:

Value	Generates
Less than 0	The same number for any given *numeric_expression*
Equal to 0	The last number generated
Greater than 0	The next random number

- If you omit *numeric_expression*, RND generates the next number in the sequence.

Example:

```
'Print ten random numbers
FOR i = 1 TO 10
    PRINT INT(RND * 10)
NEXT i
```

Related statements: RANDOMIZE

RSET Statement

Moves data into a random-access file buffer or right-justifies the value of a string variable.

Syntax:

RSET *string_variable* = *string_expression*

Notes:

■ *string_variable* is either a random-access file variable or a string variable.

■ For random-access file variables, RSET assigns a record variable of one type to another.

■ For string variables, RSET right-justifies the string.

Example:

```
DIM n AS STRING * 10
PRINT "ABCDE"
RSET n = "ABCDE"
PRINT n
```

Running this program produces the following display:

```
ABCDE
     ABCDE
```

Related statements: FIELD; LSET

RTRIM$ Function

Removes trailing spaces from a string expression.

Syntax:

RTRIM$(*string_expression*)

Notes:

■ *string_expression* is any string expression.

Example:

```
a$ = "AAAA    "
b$ = "BBBB"
PRINT RTRIM$(a$); b$
```

Running this program produces the following display:

```
AAAABBBB
```

Related functions: LTRIM$

RUN Statement

Runs the program currently in memory or an existing program from disk.

Syntax:

RUN [*line_number*]

or

RUN [*file_name*]

Notes:

■ *line_number* is a line number in the current program at which execution should begin. If you omit *line_number*, RUN begins at the first line number.

■ *file_name* is a string expression containing the name of a file to execute. QBasic assumes the BAS extension.

■ RUN closes all files and erases all variables. To share variables, use the CHAIN statement.

Example:

```
RUN "FILENAME"
```

Related statements: CHAIN

SCREEN Function

Returns the character or the color attribute for the character at the specified row and column.

Syntax:

SCREEN(*row*, *column*[, *get_color*])

Notes:

■ *row* and *column* are the coordinates of the character.

■ *get_color* is a numeric expression. If *get_color* is 1,
  SCREEN returns the color of the character. If *get_color* is
  0 or is omitted, SCREEN returns the ASCII value of the
  character at the specified position.

Example:

```
DIM scr(1 TO 25, 1 TO 80) AS INTEGER
'Store current screen contents
FOR row = 1 TO 25
    FOR column = 1 TO 80
        scr(row, column) = SCREEN(row, column)
    NEXT column
NEXT row
```

SCREEN Statement

Defines the screen characteristics.

Syntax:

SCREEN [*screen_mode*][, [*coloroff*][, [*active_page*][, *visual_page*]]]

Notes:

■ *screen_mode* is an integer expression that specifies the
  mode of operation:

Value	Mode	Adapter
0	Text	CGA, EGA, VGA, MCGA
1	320 × 200 graphics	CGA, EGA, VGA, MCGA
2	640 × 200 graphics	EGA, VGA
3	720 × 348 graphics	Hercules*
4	640 × 400 graphics	Olivetti, AT&T 6300

*The Hercules driver MSHERC.COM must be loaded.

(continued)

Continued

Value	Mode	Adapter
7	320 × 200 graphics	EGA, VGA
8	640 × 200 graphics	EGA, VGA
9	640 × 350 graphics	EGA, VGA
10	640 × 350 graphics	EGA, VGA
11	640 × 480 graphics	VGA, MCGA
12	640 × 480 graphics	VGA
13	320 × 200 graphics	VGA, MCGA

■ For specifics on video modes, see *Programmer's Guide to PC and PS/2 Video Systems* (Microsoft Press, 1987).

■ *coloroff* is a numeric expression. When true, it disables color on composite monitors. (Ignored in screen modes 2 and up.)

■ *active_page* is the video display page to which text output and graphics commands write.

■ *visual_page* is the video display page that appears on your screen.

Example:

```
SCREEN 1    '320 x 200 graphics
LINE (10, 10)-(20, 20), , B
```

Related functions: POINT

Related statements: CIRCLE; COLOR; DRAW; GET (Graphics); LINE; PAINT; PALETTE; PALETTE USING; PRESET; PSET; PUT (Graphics); VIEW; WINDOW

SEEK Function

Returns the current file pointer position.

Syntax:

SEEK(*file_number*)

Notes:

- *file_number* is the file number assigned to the file in its OPEN statement.

- For random-access files, SEEK returns a record number in the range 1 through 2,147,483,647. For binary and sequential files, SEEK returns the current byte offset.

Example:

```
position = SEEK(1)
```

Related functions: LOC

Related statements: OPEN; SEEK

SEEK Statement

Sets the file pointer position for the next read or write operation.

Syntax:

SEEK [#] *file_number, position*

Notes:

- *file_number* is the file number assigned to the file in its OPEN statement.

- *position* is the desired record number in a random-access file or the byte offset in a binary or sequential file. It must be in the range 1 to 2,147,483,647.

Example:

```
OPEN "SALARY.DAT" FOR RANDOM AS #1 LEN = 80
SEEK #1, 5          'Move pointer to record 5
```

Related functions: LOC; SEEK

Related statements: GET(File I/O); OPEN; PUT(File I/O)

SELECT CASE Statement

Evaluates an expression and executes the corresponding block of statements.

Syntax:

SELECT CASE *test_expression*
CASE *match_expression*
   [*statements*]
[**CASE** *match_expression*
   [*statements*]]
⋮
[**CASE ELSE**
   [*default_statements*]]
END SELECT

Notes:

■ The SELECT CASE statement evaluates an expression and searches the list of possible cases for a match. If a match is found, QBasic executes the statements for that case.

■ *test_expression* is a string or numeric expression to evaluate and compare to the possible cases.

■ *match_expression* is an expression to match *test_expression*. It can have the form

   expression[, *expression*]...

If any of the expressions listed match *test_expression, statements* executes.

■ *match_expression* can also take the form

   expression **TO** *expression*

This provides a range of possible values to match.

■ Lastly, *match_expression* can have the form

   IS *relation_operator expression*

where *relation_operator* is <, >, <=, >=, =, or < >.

- *statements* is the list of statements that execute for a matching case.

- *default_statements* is the list of statements that execute when no matching expression is found. These statements are associated with the CASE ELSE clause.

- After the statements within a matching case execute, the program continues execution at the first statement following the END SELECT statement.

Example:

```
FOR i = 1 TO 5
    SELECT CASE i
    CASE 1
        PRINT "One"
    CASE 2, 3
        PRINT "Two or three"
    CASE IS = 4
        PRINT "Four"
    CASE ELSE
        PRINT "Five"
    END SELECT
NEXT i
```

Running this program produces the following display:

```
One
Two or three
Two or three
Four
Five
```

Related statements: IF

SGN Function

Returns a value indicating the sign of an expression.

Syntax:

SGN(*numeric_expression*)

Notes:

- *numeric_expression* is any numeric expression. If the
  value of the expression is positive, SGN returns 1. If the
  value is negative, SGN returns −1. If the value is 0, SGN
  returns 0.

Example:

```
PRINT SGN(-3)
PRINT SGN(0)
PRINT SGN(127)
```

Running this program produces the following display:

```
-1
 0
 1
```

SHARED Statement

Gives a subprogram or function access to module-level variables.

Syntax:

SHARED *variable*[**AS** *typename*][, *variable*[**AS** *typename*]]...

Notes:

- By default, a subprogram or function has access to a variable only if you pass the variable as a parameter.

- *variable* is the name of the module-level variable to share.

- *typename* is the variable's type: INTEGER, LONG,
  SINGLE, DOUBLE, STRING, or a user-defined type.

Example:

```
DIM a AS INTEGER
a = 5
CALL Test
END
```

```
SUB Test
    SHARED a AS INTEGER
    PRINT "Value of variable A is"; a
END SUB
```

Related statements: DIM

SHELL Statement

Temporarily exits the program to execute an MS-DOS command or batch file.

Syntax:

SHELL [*MS-DOS_command*]

Notes:

■ *MS-DOS_command* is a string expression that specifies the command to execute. When the MS-DOS command completes, your program continues. If you omit *MS-DOS_command*, SHELL displays the MS-DOS prompt. When you complete your work with MS-DOS, use the MS-DOS EXIT command to resume your program.

Example:

```
SHELL "DIR"           'Display directory listing

SHELL                 'MS-DOS prompt
```

SIN Function

Returns the sine of the specified angle.

Syntax:

SIN(*angle*)

Notes:

■ *angle* is a numeric expression that specifies an angle in radians.

■ You can express angles in radians or degrees. The QBasic trigonometric routines support only radians. To convert from degrees to radians, use the following equation:

radians = 3.141593 * (*degrees* / 180)

Example:

```
pi = 3.141593
PRINT "Sine of pi", SIN(pi)
PRINT "Sine of pi/2", SIN(pi / 2)
```

Running this program produces the following display:

```
Sine of pi      -3.258414E-07
Sine of pi/2     1
```

Related statements: ATN; COS; TAN

SLEEP Statement

Suspends program execution for the specified length of time.

Syntax:

SLEEP [*seconds*]

Notes:

■ *seconds* is the number of seconds the program will be suspended.

■ The program remains suspended until the user presses a key, the specified number of seconds expires, or an event currently being trapped occurs.

■ If *seconds* is omitted or is less than 1, the program remains suspended until the user presses a key or an event currently being trapped occurs.

Example:

```
SLEEP 30
```

SOUND Statement

Generates a sound from the computer's speaker.

Syntax:

SOUND *frequency, duration*

Notes:

- *frequency* is an integer expression (from 37 through 32,767) that specifies the sound's frequency in hertz.

- *duration* is an unsigned integer expression (from 0 through 65,535) that specifies the length of the sound in clock ticks. A clock tick occurs 18.2 times per second.

Example:

```
FOR i = 37 TO 3000
     PRINT i
     SOUND i, 1
NEXT i
```

Related functions: PLAY

Related statements: BEEP; PLAY

SPACE$ Function

Returns a string containing the specified number of spaces.

Syntax:

SPACE$(*num_spaces*)

Notes:

■ *num_spaces* is an integer expression (from 0 through 32,767).

Example:

```
FOR i = 0 TO 5
    PRINT SPACE$(i); i
NEXT i
```

Running this program produces the following display:

```
0
 1
  2
   3
    4
     5
```

Related functions: SPC; TAB

SPC Function

Skips the specified number of spaces in a PRINT or LPRINT statement.

Syntax:

SPC(*num_spaces*)

Notes:

■ *num_spaces* is an integer value (from 0 through 32,767).

Example:

```
FOR i = 0 TO 5
    PRINT SPC(i); i
NEXT i
```

Related functions: SPACE$; TAB

SQR Function

Returns the square root of an expression.

Syntax:

SQR(*numeric_expression*)

Notes:

■ *numeric_expression* is any non-negative numeric expression.

Example:

```
FOR i = 0 TO 100
    PRINT i, SQR(i)
NEXT i
```

STATIC Statement

Makes the specified variable local to a subprogram or function and directs QBasic to preserve the variable's value between calls.

Syntax:

STATIC *variable*[**AS** *typename*][, *variable*[**AS** *typename*]]...

Notes:

■ *variable* is the name of the variable to make static.

■ *typename* is the variable's type: INTEGER, LONG, SINGLE, DOUBLE, STRING, or a user-defined type.

Example:

```
CALL Test
CALL Test
END

SUB Test
    STATIC a AS INTEGER
    PRINT a
    a = a + 1
END SUB
```

Running this program produces the following display:

```
0
1
```

Related statements: COMMON; SHARED

STICK Function

Returns a joystick's *x* or *y* coordinate.

Syntax:

STICK(*numeric_expression*)

Notes:

■ *numeric_expression* is an unsigned integer in the range 0 through 3 that specifies the desired value:

Value	Returns
0	*x* coordinate of joystick A
1	*y* coordinate of joystick A
2	*x* coordinate of joystick B
3	*y* coordinate of joystick B

■ *x* and *y* coordinates can range from 1 through 200.

Example:

```
x% = STICK(0)
y% = STICK(1)
```

STOP Statement

Ends the program at any point.

Syntax:

STOP

Notes:

■ A program should have only one starting and ending point. The use of STOP to end a program from different locations is strongly discouraged.

Example:

```
Handler:
    PRINT "Failed to open file on"
    PRINT "the third attempt"
    STOP
```

STR$ Function

Returns the string representation of a numeric expression.

Syntax:

STR$(*numeric_expression*)

Notes:

■ *numeric_expression* is any numeric expression.

Example:

```
x$ = STR$(3.2718)
PRINT x$
```

Related functions: VAL

STRIG Function

Returns the status of a joystick trigger.

Syntax:

STRIG(*numeric_expression*)

Notes:

■ *numeric_expression* is an unsigned integer (from 0 through 7) that specifies the type of information desired:

Value	Condition
0	Lower joystick A button pressed since last STRIG(0)
1	Lower joystick A button currently pressed
2	Lower joystick B button pressed since last STRIG(2)
3	Lower joystick B button currently pressed
4	Upper joystick A button pressed since last STRIG(4)
5	Upper joystick A button currently pressed
6	Upper joystick B button pressed since last STRIG(6)
7	Upper joystick B button currently pressed

■ If the specified condition is true, STRIG returns −1; otherwise, STRIG returns 0.

Example:

```
'Wait for user to press
'the lower button of joystick A
DO
LOOP UNTIL STRIG(0)
```

Related statements: ON *event* GOSUB; STRIG

STRIG Statements

Enable or disable joystick trapping.

Syntax:

STRIG(*button*) **ON**

or

STRIG(*button*) **OFF**

or

STRIG(*button*) **STOP**

Notes:

■ *button* is a numeric expression that specifies which joystick button to trap:

Value	Traps
0	Lower button on joystick A
2	Lower button on joystick B
4	Upper button on joystick A
6	Upper button on joystick B

■ STRIG(*button*) ON enables joystick trapping for the specified button.

■ STRIG(*button*) OFF disables joystick trapping for the specified button. All events are ignored.

■ STRIG(*button*) STOP temporarily disables joystick trapping for the specified button. Events are processed once trapping is enabled.

Example:

```
ON STRIG(0) GOSUB Handler
STRIG(0) ON
```

Related functions: STRIG

Related statements: ON *event* GOSUB

STRING$ Function

Returns a string containing the specified number of occur-rences of a character.

Syntax:

STRING$(*num_char*, *ascii_character*)

or

STRING$(*num_char*, *string_expression*)

Notes:

■ *num_char* is the desired number of occurrences of a char-acter.

■ *ascii_character* is the ASCII code of the character.

■ *string_expression* is any string expression. If you provide a string, STRING$ uses the first character of the string.

Example:

```
a$ = STRING$(10, 65)
PRINT a$
```

SUB Statement

Declares a Basic subprogram.

Syntax:

SUB *subprogram_name* [(*parameter_list*)] [**STATIC**]
  ⋮
END SUB

Notes:

■ *subprogram_name* is the name of the subprogram (up to 40 characters).

■ *parameter_list* is a list of parameters in the following form:

variable[()][**AS** *typename*][, *variable*[()][**AS** *typename*]]...

■ The keyword STATIC directs QBasic to retain the value of the subprogram's local variables between calls.

Example:

```
CALL Test (1, 5.5, "TEST")
END

SUB Test (a AS INTEGER, b AS SINGLE, c AS STRING)
    PRINT a, b, c
END SUB
```

Related statements: CALL; DECLARE; END; EXIT; GOSUB

SWAP Statement

Exchanges the values of two variables.

Syntax:

SWAP *variable1*, *variable2*

Notes:

■ *variable1* and *variable2* must be the same type.

Example:

```
a = 1
b = 2
SWAP a, b
PRINT a, b
```

Running this program produces the following display:

2   1

SYSTEM Statement

Ends the program and returns control to the operating system.

Syntax:

SYSTEM

Notes:

■ SYSTEM closes all open files and ends the program's execution.

Example:

SYSTEM

TAB Function

Moves the print position to the specified column.

Syntax:

TAB(*column*)

Notes:

■ *column* is the desired tab column. If the current position is beyond the specified column, TAB moves to the column on the next line.

Example:

```
FOR i = 1 TO 10
    PRINT TAB(i); i
NEXT i
```

Related functions: SPC

TAN Function

Returns the tangent of the specified angle.

Syntax:

TAN(*angle*)

Notes:

■ *angle* is a numeric expression that specifies an angle in radians.

■ You can express an angle in radians or degrees. The QBasic trigonometric routines support only radians. To convert from degrees to radians, use the following equation:

radians = 3.141593 ∗ (*degrees* / 180)

Example:

```
pi = 3.141593
PRINT TAN(pi / 4)
```

Related functions: ATN; COS; SIN

TIME$ Function

Returns an 8-character string containing the current system time in the form *hh:mm:ss*.

Syntax:

TIME$

Example:

```
PRINT TIME$
```

Running this program line at noon produces the following display:

```
12:00:00
```

Related functions: DATE$

Related statements: DATE$; TIME$

TIME$ Statement

Sets the system time.

Syntax:

TIME$ = *string_expression*

Notes:

- *string_expression* is a string expression containing the desired time in the form "*hh:mm:ss*" where *hh* is the hour (0 through 23), *mm* is the minutes (0 through 59), and *ss* is the seconds (0 through 59).

- TIME$ allows you to specify only hours; hours and minutes; or hours, minutes, and seconds.

Examples:

```
TIME$ = "12"
TIME$ = "12:30"
```

Related functions: DATE$; TIME$

Related statements: DATE$

TIMER Function

Returns the number of seconds since midnight.

Syntax:

TIMER

Notes:

■ You can use TIMER with the RANDOMIZE statement to seed the random number generator.

Example:

```
RANDOMIZE TIMER
```

TIMER Statements

Enable or disable timer event trapping.

Syntax:

TIMER ON

or

TIMER OFF

or

TIMER STOP

Notes:

■ TIMER ON enables timer event trapping.

■ TIMER OFF disables timer event trapping. Timer events that occur are ignored.

■ TIMER STOP temporarily suspends timer event trapping. Events that occur are processed after trapping is enabled.

Example:

```
ON TIMER(10) GOSUB Handler
TIMER ON
DO
LOOP UNTIL INKEY$ <> ""
END

Handler:
    PRINT TIME$
    RETURN
```

Related statements: ON *event* GOSUB

TROFF Statement

Disables tracing of statements.

Syntax:

TROFF

Notes:

■ TROFF and TRON are debugging tools used by older Basic systems. You will usually find that using the QBasic debugging tools is more convenient.

Example:

```
TROFF
```

Related statements: TRON

TRON Statement

Enables tracing of statements.

Syntax:

TRON

Notes:

See TROFF

Example:

TRON

Related statements: TROFF

TYPE Statement

Creates a user-defined type.

Syntax:

TYPE *user_typename*
    element_name **AS** *typename*
    ⋮
END TYPE

Notes:

- *user_typename* is the name of the user-defined type.

- *element_name* is the name of an element in a record.

- *typename* is the element's type: INTEGER, LONG, SINGLE, DOUBLE, fixed-length string (for example, STRING ∗ 4), or another user-defined type.

- TYPE creates a template for future variable declarations. To create a variable of this type, you must use DIM, REDIM, COMMON, STATIC, or SHARED.

Example:

```
TYPE Employee
    ename AS STRING * 20
    salary AS SINGLE
END TYPE

DIM emp AS Employee
```

```
emp.ename = "Stephanie"
emp.salary = 30000
PRINT emp.ename, emp.salary
```

Running this program produces the following display:

```
Stephanie 30000
```

Related statements: COMMON; DIM; REDIM; SHARED; STATIC

UBOUND Function

Returns the highest array subscript for the specified array dimension.

Syntax:

UBOUND(*array_name*[, *dimension*])

Notes:

■ *array-name* is the name of the array of interest.

■ *dimension* is an integer value specifying the dimension of interest in a multidimensional array. The default is 1.

Example:

```
DIM a(1 TO 5, 1 TO 10, 1 TO 25)
PRINT UBOUND(a), UBOUND(a, 2), UBOUND(a, 3)
```

Running this program produces the following display:

```
5       10      25
```

Related functions: LBOUND

Related statements: DIM; OPTION BASE; REDIM

UCASE$ Function

Returns a character string with all letters in the specified
string expression in uppercase characters.

Syntax:

UCASE$(*string_expression*)

Notes:

■ *string_expression* is any string expression.

Example:

```
a$ = "aBcd#F"
PRINT UCASE$(a$)
```

Running this program produces the following display:

ABCD#F

Related functions: LCASE$

UNLOCK Statement

Unlocks portions of a shared file for access by other network
programs.

Syntax:

UNLOCK [#]*file_number*[, {*record* ¦ [*start*] **TO** *end*}]

Notes:

■ *file_number* is the file number assigned to the file in its
OPEN statement.

■ *record* is an integer value that specifies a single record to
release in a random-access file or a single byte to unlock
in a binary file.

- *start* and *end* are integer values that specify the range of record numbers to release in a random-access file or the range of bytes to unlock in a binary file.

- UNLOCK is necessary only in network environments.

Example:

```
OPEN "SHARED.DAT" FOR RANDOM AS #1
LOCK #1, 1 TO 10
'Perform file update operations
UNLOCK #1, 1 TO 10
CLOSE #1
```

Related statements: LOCK

VAL Function

Converts a string representation of a numeric value to the actual numeric value.

Syntax:

VAL(*string_expression*)

Notes:

- *string_expression* is the string representation of a numeric value.

- VAL stops at the first character it cannot recognize as part of a number. Valid characters are 0 through 9, the period (.), the minus sign (−), and the plus sign (+).

Example:

```
PRINT VAL("33.44")
PRINT VAL("88k")
```

Running this program produces the following display:

```
33.44
88
```

Related functions: STR$

VARPTR Function

Returns a variable's offset in memory.

Syntax:

VARPTR(*variable*)

Notes:

■ *variable* is the name of any variable in your program.

■ QBasic does not guarantee that a variable will reside in the same memory location throughout the program execution. Use VARPTR immediately before any code that uses the offset value.

Example:

See CALL ABSOLUTE

Related functions: VARSEG

Related statements: DEF SEG

VARPTR$ Function

Returns a string representation of a variable's offset for use in the PLAY and DRAW statements.

Syntax:

VARPTR$(*string_variable*)

Notes:

■ *string_variable* is a string variable containing DRAW or PLAY commands.

■ QBasic does not guarantee that a variable will reside in
the same memory location throughout the program execution. Use VARPTR$ immediately before any code that
uses the address.

Example:

```
scale$ = "CDEFGAB"
PLAY "X" + VARPTR$(scale$)
```

Related statements: DRAW; PLAY

VARSEG Function

Returns a variable's segment in memory.

Syntax:

VARSEG(*variable*)

Notes:

■ *variable* is the name of any variable in your program.

Example:

See CALL ABSOLUTE

Related functions: VARPTR

Related statements: DEF SEG

VIEW Statement

Defines the screen coordinates within which graphics can be
displayed.

Syntax:

VIEW [[**SCREEN**] (*x1, y1*)-(*x2, y2*)[, [*fill_color*][, *border_present*]]]

Notes:

- VIEW allows you to restrict graphics output to specific co-ordinates on the screen. Coordinates outside this range are not drawn.

- The keyword SCREEN states that graphics coordinates are relative to the screen, not to the viewport.

- $x1$ and $y1$ are the coordinates of one corner of the viewport; $x2$ and $y2$ are the coordinates of the opposite corner.

- *fill_color* specifies the color with which to fill the viewport.

- *border_present* is any numeric expression that, when present, directs VIEW to draw a border around the viewport.

- If you omit all arguments, VIEW sets the viewport to the entire screen.

- The SCREEN and RUN statements set the viewport back to the entire screen.

Example:

```
SCREEN 1
VIEW (0, 0)-(20, 20), 1, 2
LINE (10, 10)-(100, 100)
```

Related statements: CLS; SCREEN; WINDOW

VIEW PRINT Statement

Defines the text mode scrolling region.

Syntax:

VIEW PRINT [*top_row* **TO** *bottom_row*]

Notes:

- *top_row* and *bottom_row* are integer values that specify the top and bottom rows of the text mode scrolling region.

- If you omit all arguments, VIEW PRINT sets the scrolling region to the entire screen.

Example:

```
CLS
VIEW PRINT 5 TO 10
FOR i = 1 TO 100
    PRINT i, i, i, i
NEXT i
```

Related statements: CLS; LOCATE; PRINT

WAIT Statement

Suspends program execution until the specified bit pattern is read from an input port.

Syntax:

WAIT *port_number*, *AND_expression*[, *XOR_expression*]

Notes:

- *port_number* is an integer expression (from 0 through 255) that identifies the port.

- *AND_expression* is an integer expression that WAIT combines with the port value using an AND operation.

- *XOR_expression* is an integer expression that WAIT combines with the port value using an XOR operation.

- Data from the specified port is first combined with *XOR_expression* if supplied. The result is then combined with *AND_expression*. If the result is zero, WAIT continues reading port values; otherwise, QBasic executes the next statement.

Example:

```
WAIT 45, 64
```

WHILE/WEND Statement

Repeats a set of statements as long as a specified condition is true.

Syntax:

WHILE *condition*
    [*statements*]
WEND

Notes:

■ *condition* is a Boolean expression. As long as *condition* is true, QBasic executes the statements within the loop.

■ *statements* is any list of statements.

■ WHILE/WEND is an older looping construct. The use of DO is preferred.

Example:

```
i = 0
WHILE i < 100
     PRINT i
     i = i + 1
WEND
```

Related statements: DO UNTIL; DO WHILE; EXIT

WIDTH Statement

Sets the number of columns on the screen or other device or sets the width of a file.

Syntax:

WIDTH [*columns*][, *lines*]

or

WIDTH #*file_number*, *columns*

or

WIDTH *device_name*, *columns*

or

WIDTH LPRINT *columns*

Notes:

■ *columns* is the number of columns. The value must be 40 or 80 for the screen.

■ *lines* is the number of rows of text that appear on the screen. The value can be 25, 30, 43, 50, or 60, depending on your display adapter and current screen mode.

■ *file_number* is the file number assigned to the file in its OPEN statement.

■ *device_name* is a string expression that contains the name of the desired device.

■ The keyword LPRINT sets the number of columns for the printer.

■ After you specify a width for a device, output statements automatically wrap output to the next line when the width is exceeded.

Example:

```
'EGA monitor
WIDTH 80, 43
FOR i = 1 TO 100
    PRINT i
NEXT i
```

Related statements: LPRINT; LPRINT USING; PRINT; PRINT USING; SCREEN

WINDOW Statement

Defines the logical coordinates for the current viewport.

Syntax:

WINDOW [[**SCREEN**] (*x1*, *y1*)-(*x2*, *y2*)]

Notes:

■ The keyword SCREEN inverts the screen's coordinate system such that *y* values increase in value from the top to the bottom of the screen.

■ The coordinates *x1*, *y1* and *x2*, *y2* specify the logical coordinates of the viewport.

Example:

```
SCREEN 1
WINDOW (0, 0)-(50, 50)
LINE (10, 10)-(40, 40), 2, B
```

Related statements: CLS; SCREEN; VIEW

WRITE Statement

Writes data to the screen or a sequential file.

Syntax:

WRITE [[#]*file_number*,]*expression_list*

Notes:

■ *file_number* is the file number assigned to the file in its OPEN statement. If you omit *file_number*, QBasic writes the data to the screen.

■ *expression_list* is a list of one or more variables or expressions separated by commas.

■ WRITE places a comma between each expression in the file; the PRINT statement does not.

Example:

```
OPEN "TEST.DAT" FOR OUTPUT AS #1
WRITE #1, "TEST", 5, 3.21, "END"
CLOSE #1
```

Running this program produces the following result in TEST.DAT:

```
"TEST",5,3.21,"END"
```

Related statements: PRINT

Keywords Not Supported in QBasic

QuickBasic

ALIAS	Interrupt
BYVAL	InterruptX
CDECL	LOCAL
COMMAND$	SADD
EVENT	SETMEM
$INCLUDE	SIGNAL
Int86	UEVENT
Int86x	

GW-BASIC/BASICA

AUTO	LOAD
CONT	MERGE
DEF USR	MOTOR
DELETE	NEW
EDIT	RENUM
LIST	SAVE
LLIST	USR

APPENDIX B

Statement and Function Summary

ON *expression* Statements

OPEN Statement

OPTION BASE Statement

OUT Statement

PAINT Statement

PALETTE Statement

PALETTE USING Statement

PCOPY Statement

PEEK Function

PEN Function

PEN Statements

PLAY Function

PLAY Statement

PLAY Statements (Event Trapping)

PMAP Function

POINT Function

POKE Statement

POS Function

PRESET Statement

PRINT Statement

PRINT USING Statement

PSET Statement

PUT Statement (File I/O)

PUT Statement (Graphics)

RANDOMIZE Statement

READ Statement

REDIM Statement

REM Statement

RESET Statement

RESTORE Statement

RESUME Statement

RETURN Statement

RIGHT$ Function

RMDIR Statement

RND Function

RSET Statement

RTRIM$ Function

RUN Statement

SCREEN Function

SCREEN Statement

SEEK Function

SEEK Statement

SELECT CASE Statement

SGN Function

SHARED Statement

SHELL Statement

SIN Function

SLEEP Statement

SOUND Statement

SPACE$ Function

SPC Function

SQR Function

STATIC Statement

STICK Function

STOP Statement

STR$ Function

STRIG Function

STRIG Statements

STRING$ Function

SUB Statement

SWAP Statement

SYSTEM Statement

TAB Function

TAN Function

TIME$ Function

TIME$ Statement

TIMER Function

TIMER Statements

TROFF Statement

TRON Statement
TYPE Statement

UBOUND Function
UCASE$ Function
UNLOCK Statement

VAL Function
VARPTR Function
VARPTR$ Function

VARSEG Function
VIEW Statement
VIEW PRINT Statement

WAIT Statement
WHILE/WEND Statement
WIDTH Statement
WINDOW Statement
WRITE Statement

APPENDIX C

Scan Codes

Key	Code	Key	Code	Key	Code
Esc	1	A	30	F1	59
! or 1	2	S	31	F2	60
@ or 2	3	D	32	F3	61
# or 3	4	F	33	F4	62
$ or 4	5	G	34	F5	63
% or 5	6	H	35	F6	64
^ or 6	7	J	36	F7	65
& or 7	8	K	37	F8	66
* or 8	9	L	38	F9	67
(or 9	10	: or ;	39	F10	68
) or 0	11	" or '	40	F11	133
_ or -	12	~ or `	41	F12	134
+ or =	13	Left Shift	42	Num Lock	69
Backspace	14		or \	43	Scroll Lock	70
Tab	15	Z	44	Home or 7	71
Q	16	X	45	Up or 8	72
W	17	C	46	PgUp or 9	73
E	18	V	47	Gray −	74
R	19	B	48	Left or 4	75
T	20	N	49	Center or 5	76
Y	21	M	50	Right or 6	77
U	22	< or ,	51	Gray +	78
I	23	> or .	52	End or 1	79
O	24	? or /	53	Down or 2	80
P	25	Right Shift	54	PgDn or 3	81
{ or [	26	PrtSc or *	55	Ins or 0	82
} or]	27	Alt	56	Del or .	83
Enter	28	Spacebar	57		
Ctrl	29	Caps Lock	58		